Made
to
Praise Him

Finding My Song

Fr. Bill Quinlivan

Made to Praise Him
© 2014 by Fr. Bill Quinlivan
All rights reserved.

Nihil Obstat and *Imprimatur:*
Most Reverend Richard J. Malone
Bishop, Diocese of Buffalo, New York
September 30, 2013

Cover & Interior Music Graphic: 123rf.com stock photo/seamartini
Photography: Used by permission
Cover Design: Elizabeth E. Little, Hyliian Graphics
Interior Formatting: The Author's Mentor,
                 www.LittleRoniPublishers.com

ISBN-13: 978-1502415127
ISBN-10: 1502415127
Also in eBook

PUBLISHED IN THE UNITED STATES OF AMERICA

DEDICATION

This book is dedicated to my first teachers of faith, Irish storytelling and music, my parents, Jim and "Kass" Quinlivan. And to the members of the first choir I ever belonged to, the Quinlivan Kids, Pat, Sue, Eileen, Joe and Mary. Family and parish church are the places where I first found "my song"!

THANK YOU

All those who have encouraged me to write, sing and play music. All those who prayed I would find my priestly vocation. Thanks to my proof-readers, Mary Quinlivan, Eileen Moriarty, Fr. Joseph Bertha and Fr. Richard Delzingaro, CRSP, Mary Rozak and Mary Ellen Zablocki. And also to my theological reader, Fr. Peter Drilling.

Contents

Foreword

One of the many fascinating icons of Our Lord and Savior Jesus Christ is the "Reader of Human Hearts." The salient feature of this particular image is the compelling depiction of the eyes. The right eye of our God focuses directly at the viewer, and represents the eye of righteousness and judgment. While the left eye looks off into the distance, mercifully seeking the return of the Prodigal, filled with joy over the return of a sinner. Both eyes form the gaze of Our Lord's vision, depicted as simultaneously righteous and mercy. Whereas the icon shows the triumph of mercy over judgment.

This unique feature of the holy icon literally depicts the manner in which Our Lord searches our lives, our deeds, yes into our very souls. He is continually, never sleeping, looking, and peering at his creation seeking to find the image of his mercy.

Father Bill Quinlivan through this autobiographical work has provided not only glimpses, but insights through his recounting of many events in his life. In his own inimitable way he opens our vision to the gaze of Jesus' mercy in his personal history of the realization of his priestly vocation, sharing some of the wonderful people he has encountered along his journey.

May you also become a reader of human hearts by reading and imitating the many whimsical, sometimes sorrowful, but always enlightening perceptions into the manifestation of God's fathomless mercy in Father Bill's personal story, and told to this world which so desperately needs it!

Father Joseph Bertha, Ph.D.

Made to Praise Him

❧ ❧ ❧ ❧ ❧ ❧

Some were born to rule a country,
Sit upon a throne
Some are made to doctor sickness,
To mend the broken bone
Others dream of fame and fortune,
Or dancing on the moon.
I just sing for Jesus' glory with every silly tune…

I was made to praise Him, I was made to praise Him,
I was made to praise Him, now and forever more!!

You were born for God's own purpose,
Your life is a gift.
Ask Him to reveal your calling,
The mystery veil to lift.
But no matter which vocation is calling you by name,
Heaven is a praise-a-thon, our eternal call's the same

You were made to praise Him…
We were made to praise Him…
Now and forever more!

Chapter One

MADE TO PRAISE HIM

As my 40th birthday approached in the year 2000, I was part of a ministry team about to work a weekend retreat for Catholic teenagers. In a moment of Olympic-sized déjà-vu, the event would be at the Catholic high school from which I graduated over two decades earlier at age seventeen. Because of my birthday ending in zero, I was asked to preach at the closing Mass, celebrated at center court of the school gym where I had some of the most humiliating moments of my youth. Gym was my least favorite class. Religion class was a piece of cake, but gym was my personal hell. Only about ten yards away was the stage, where I had some of the best fun of my teen years in plays and musicals.

When I look back over my life and see God's mighty hand at work, I'm totally convinced that a sense of humor is essential to any important moment of self-awareness. As I wrote **Made to Praise Him**, I tried to put myself back into the awkward teen years. (Which, for me, would be followed by my awkward twenties, not-so-bad thirties, and finally fine forties. The fifties just began a few years ago, but now I'm at

1

the age where I've already forgotten part of them, so it's a new kind of adventure in aging!)

Throughout my young life, certainly my parents, teachers and preachers told me that God would have a purpose for me. What I didn't realize is that every purpose under Heaven would also be a chance to *turn, turn, turn* inward and find my calling, my giftedness that could be useful for the Lord. There were many varieties of dreams and aspirations, and the endless menu was often overwhelming. Besides, how do you figure out which dreams are foolish fantasy and which are realistic? On the other hand, I'm part of the generation that watched Neil Armstrong walk on the moon. We were allowed to aim for the sky, but left to figure out which hopes are lunar and which are just plain loony.

There was a popular music group in the 1970's called The New Seekers. Honestly, while I never purchased one of their records and I was born just a few years too late to be able to list their hit songs, I can see now that I had to *become* a seeker to be a finder. And…thanks to God's magnificently mysterious and often hilarious plan, the finder is now a keeper, the one who sometimes felt like a "loser" now is only a "weeper" in the profound joy of finding my calling, my vocation. It was anything but a direct or easy path to discover what my maker had in mind. Many turns, a few traffic jams, and some flights of fancy were all included.

Birds Learn to Fly

In the daily life of my childhood, as the fourth-born of six children of Jim and Kass Quinlivan, I don't remember a lot of pressure to know and claim at a young age what I wanted to be as an adult. In my experience, the short-term goals (Getting from 4th to 5th Grade, for example. Getting from September to Christmas vacation-- a better example!) were enough to handle. Surrounded by siblings, home was a wonderfully safe place. Being one hundred and ten per cent Irish, (which means, all heritage roots in Ireland **and** growing up in South Buffalo where that nationality was the majority) faith, laughter and music were always bountiful in our home.

Growing up as part of a big family, there's an environment of sharing that sometimes challenges any sense that something is uniquely yours. All six of the Quinlivan kids could sing, and every one of us has a share in my father's dry humor as well as Mom's more outrageous wit. She belonged to what they called "The Club"-- a group of about 12 friends who met in grammar school and literally remained close until death. From that wonderful generation before TV and internet, they were a beautiful example of faithful friends. From time to time, a well-meaning member would suggest that they play cards or take up a craft together. Those attempts failed, for they had such a riot talking and telling stories that the poker chips would get stale, the glue would dry while they talked all night. Each "Club" member took turns hosting their get-togethers, and from our bedrooms upstairs, they could be heard laughing so loudly downstairs when we were in bed on a school night that we *had* to sneak down to the landing to try to hear what was so funny. More often than not, the outbursts of laughter were followed by an incredulous cry from one of the ladies: "Kass!!!"

Families seem to collect a cache of stories about each child that can be pulled out of the files should they need to be humbled. (I've decided to write this book before my siblings got any idea to do so, for it's better to humble yourself before others can)! As years go by, certain narratives of family history take on a life of their own to the point where the next generation wonders how so many people could recall such vivid detail about seemingly insignificant incidents.

The following story about little Billy Quinlivan was not only told at my mother's Club (as well as playing in re-runs for decades in family lore) but found its way to print in Reader's Digest's *Life In These United States* feature. (My Aunt, Sister Mary Kathleen, scored the $25 or whatever it paid back in the mid-Sixties)! The story begins when a four-year old me found a dead sparrow in the back yard on a hot summer day in Buffalo. (For those of you unfamiliar with Buffalo, hot Summer days are real. We do have beautiful summers but like family legends, our snowstorms and blizzards get more publicity…) Mom glanced out the picture window in our dining room at one point to see me throwing the dead bird into the air. She hurried around to the back porch to get a better view of her son throwing a lifeless creature into the air, only to have it fall to the grass with a light thud. And then, as the story goes, she heard me say with great desperation: "C'mon birdie, *fly*… or Daddy's gonna *bury* you!!!" Obviously, at my preschool age, I'd had very little experience of death. I preferred to think that I had already accepted by faith the Gospel message of resurrection. This Lazarus with wings was, alas, not to return to the living. It wasn't that I didn't try.

Actually, I was always quite naïve. That's no exaggeration. I bought the Santa Claus and Easter Bunny story big time. On Christmas Eve, I laid awake expecting to hear reindeer hooves, and was more often than not more fixated on trying to witness Santa's landing and take-off than the pile of toys that he left. The Bunny was another story. He actually terrified me, because the person at the Seneca Mall in Easter Bunny costume with that big, fake head didn't speak. The department store Santas were obviously human beings (with magic power, but human nonetheless…) But I was freaked out by no "Ho-Ho-Ho" from the basket-bringing beast. His silence made me wonder just what he was thinking. Thankfully, there were no legends of his knowing how well or poorly we behaved, no threat of coal instead of chocolate. And I guess I reasoned that the Bunny was Catholic, since he celebrated Easter. But in my imagination, I sometimes shuddered in fear that he would not only hide our baskets but be hiding somewhere in the house, too. At times, I'd pray that Jesus would rise on Easter and rid the house of this odd-looking animal. Of course, I never offered to let him take the chocolate back. And there was a strange Easter morning satisfaction in biting his brother bunny's ears off, so that it would protect us and deter that hopping houseguest for at least until the next year.

Being innocent is such a precious part of childhood. But at a certain age, it becomes known as naïve. I did actually think that Mount Rushmore was a natural formation. Actually I attributed it to God's artwork; His creative expression on a mountainside for Americans to enjoy. Heck—if He could make the whole world and He could carve ten commandments into stone, why not give us a presidential portrait on a precipice? That kind of innocence eventually faded, but I do try to keep a few seeds of it stored away in the hopeful, imaginative "anything is possible" part of my heart. When people scoff and call me naïve today, I just quietly say to myself: "It *looked* like the sparrow in the yard was playing possum … Someone had to give him a chance to fly again…the Easter Bunny told me so!"

Stepping Out for a Breath of Incense

At the age of eleven, my best friend, Ray Donohue (who lived across the street and had a dog-- life-long wish of mine...) casually asked me if I'd like to attend the Novena at church on Monday night. I had gotten to know Ray when my 6th Grade teacher, Sr. Jane Muldoon, started the Junior Legion of Mary. He was a legion member, though two years older than I. A small group of kids would stay after school and pray on Monday afternoons. It felt like a very natural thing to do. My brother Joe joined, too. But attending a

Novena never crossed my mind. I don't know if I had even heard the word novena, for it sounded like what our Italian neighbors said when they were out of wine: oh, wait, that's no vino!

I did accept the invitation to the novena, which included prayers to Our Lady of the Miraculous Medal, but I didn't join Ray serving on the altar, as I had yet to be trained. But this night in 1972 made an indelible impression on me as it was my first experience of Eucharistic Adoration! Though the exposition of the Blessed Sacrament was relatively brief, something in me felt strongly drawn to that presence of Jesus. It was different from attending Mass; a beautiful devotion with incense, hymns, prayers. And afterwards, an elderly couple, Mr. and Mrs. Park, invited us to their house for dessert. They were saints, actually, and became like my grandparents until the day they died.

Novena night became a weekly ritual, and soon I was working Bingo on Fridays and Saturdays and joined the choir. At age eleven, I was involved in everything a kid could do at church. While the whole family attended weekly Mass, I was the only member so deeply involved in parish life. It became part of my identity, and my passion—an extended family. Years later, Ray would enter the seminary and get ordained. I had thought about priesthood especially in late grammar school when a lot of my time was spent serving at Church. But by the time I was sophomore in high school, Ray graduated and moved away to seminary. While he and I often shared the dream of becoming a priest, when I started getting involved in other activities like high school musicals, I met many other people my age who did not have that calling. And when not singing in the choir, I began to enjoy singing on stage. I eventually concluded that my "dream" would be in the entertainment world. This seemed to be what God made me for, as making music gave me such joy! Ray could be the priest...I would be the star!! Sounds more than a little naïve—what did I tell you??

While I enjoyed the stage experience, I was never the choice of the directors for much more than chorus roles. And choreographers usually began to arrange our positions in a number with "Tall kids in the back!" ("Rats!' **Why** did I eat those vegetables?!?!'")

My very first audition for a musical was a disaster. Every person trying out was told to sing the "Battle Hymn of the Republic," which I of course knew from Church—we sang it on the Sunday before the Fourth of July! When the accompanists started to play, it was in a key that was too high for me. Being a polite, naïve and shy, I just tried my best, but it was completely out of the range of my voice. I never thought about it then, but I had never sung alone accompanied by an instrument, and was used to just starting wherever I felt comfortable. I often just sang around the house (Even while scrubbing the back hall stairs, my Saturday chore. I not only knew the words to *A Spoonful of Sugar* from *Mary Poppins* but ascribed to that philosophy to make the dirty work fun. By the time I finished the bottom stair, I could have swept up all the sugar I sang over the now-clean floor)!

A few days after my first stage audition, the day the cast list was posted and my name wasn't on it, I was shocked and very disappointed. Deep down, I knew that I could sing.

My family used to sing in the car on long rides, but it was always a capella. I would be singing constantly as a child. Not just funeral songs for sparrows in the yard but every Christmas carol I knew and the entire score of "Sound of Music." My siblings knew that movie soundtrack, too. Mom used to have the six of us get up and sing selections from the film story of the Von Trapp Family for company. Usually, it was when we had nuns for dinner. (That is, as guests…not the entree. Mom's older sister was a Sister of Mercy, Sr. M. Kathleen, and in that era sisters never travelled alone). Six became five when my brother Pat got too cool (he felt more than a little *von-Trapped*) and his theme song became "So, Long, Farewell." I, on the other hand just kept singing "Cuck-Coo" and loving it.

To this day, when I try to sing and realize that my voice can no longer hit the same notes Julie Andrews and I as a boy soprano could reach, I am very grateful to Fr. Peter Cheppitis, OFM.

He taught Religion at Bishop Timon High School, and helped direct the musicals. Fr. Peter pulled me aside the day that day the musical cast list went up with my name missing, and explained very kindly that they noticed my voice was still changing. And had they let me into the show I could strain it and ruin my voice for good. I should wait a year and try out again. Then he asked me to be a Production Assistant on the show, which I did. It probably saved my voice for God's later purposes. Not singing is sometimes more important than singing. Waiting and growing are always part of life's songbook.

Fr. Kilian's Cockroach

In my youth when I wasn't doing my chores or pretending that I was Dick Van Dyke as Burt, the chimney sweep on the rooftops of London, I was getting more involved in the life of the Church. I imagined my parents felt it's not a bad place for a kid to spend his time. And it would "keep me out of trouble" as parents like to say.

About 1972, a young priest was sent to St. Teresa's Church as an assistant. My brother Joe and I had finally taken altar server training, and we both liked Fr. John Kilian from the start. He never seemed to be in a hurry like the pastor and other priests. (Now that I'm a pastor, I do understand them much better)! And Fr. Kilian had a great sense of humor. Sometimes after Mass, he'd call us over and say "Boys...I have something very important to tell you....words of wisdom...." and then he would belch. These were the days before girl servers. The boys just roared: "How cool is that, a priest who burps!!!" Joe and I would laugh all the way home.

Fr. Kilian was a product of his times. He was ordained in the late 1960's and his hair was just a bit longer than any kid in our Catholic school could wear it. He was a wonderful preacher and very serious about his duties. But I found in him an approachable humanity, actually, the first priest I ever knew as a person and, over time, as a friend. Looking back, those early days of knowing him were very important to my understanding of what a priest was and did. Besides his gift of humor, he showed us kids respect and seemed interested in who we were. He could easily segue into our conversations about the mundane and everyday to sharing his experiences of Jesus. There was something I admired in that, wishing to be able to learn how to speak of my faith and integrate it into my daily life.

In the early 1970s, our aging pastor was not very taken with the younger priests who were coming along. In fact, most assistants didn't last long. Parishioners would remark that the rectory should install a revolving door to facilitate the number of young priests coming and going. Fr. Kilian stayed about two years, a bit of a record, and that was probably God's response to our prayers. As I said earlier, he was a bit quirky in a 60's kind of way. He was also what they call a pack rat, and had a pile of old New York Times Sunday magazines in his room. During the Second Vatican Council, they said that the most "relevant" preachers would have the Church's latest teachings/ documents of the council in one hand and a newspaper in the other.

Unfortunately, groovy young priests aren't the only ones who like old newspapers. Cockroaches do, too. And early one morning, the cranky pastor was shuffling toward his bathroom at the rectory in bare feet and "found" a crunch-

roach beneath his foot! One phone call to the bishop later, and Fr. Kilian was transferred. He asked Ray and me to help him move, and we were glad to help but sad to see him go. In our child-like reaction, we griped that we wished the pastor would be transferred instead. Years later, we'd both be priests and also pastors, and see just how reality is often different from an innocent child's hopes. Actually, we helped Fr. John move a few more times in the next several years. After some frustration with the "generation gap" in the post-Vatican II era, Fr. Kilian signed up to be a Maryknoll missionary priest for a five-year term in Bolivia.

My priest friend and I kept in touch through letter-writing, and he always told me that my letters brought him laughter and joy. Once, however, a bit of my cartoon art work on the outside of the Air Mail envelope (a dead cockroach with an "X" in his eye to show his condition) brought the attention of Bolivian customs and police. It seems that there was a rebel group in that country whose symbol was... you guessed it... a dead cockroach! And suspicious security forces are not interested in throwing a dead cockroach up in the air to see if it comes back to life...

My friendship with Fr. Kilian continued for almost forty years. We exchanged Christmas cards and occasionally ran into each other at church functions. I cherish my photos of myself with him at my ordination in 1995. And several years later, I visited him several times when he was confined to a nursing home. My second-last visit with him was very pleasant as we reminisced about the years that he was at St. Teresa's, and I was his altar server. We remembered the missionary years and run-in with the Bolivian post office inspectors. At one point in his time in Bolivia, the people of the village whom he was serving were celebrating some kind of feast. There was a tradition where the men of the village took turns running and jumping over a bonfire. They encouraged him to take part in this ritual, and when he did, unfortunately there was someone also approaching the fire from the other side. A mid-air collision left him badly injured. Months went by without my receiving a letter, then I eventually heard from him again.

A few days before he died, I felt a strong nudge from God to visit him and will always be glad that I did. This happens from time to time, where the Holy Spirit gives us a sign that we can sometimes miss. It may have even been early on Holy Thursday, the day our Catholic family commemorates the gift of priestly ministry and the sacrament of the Holy Eucharist.

My last visit to Fr. Kilian was bittersweet, as he was heavily medicated and unable to communicate much. What struck me was that, as celibates, priests can sometimes end up in these facilities in their last days. I stayed for a while and prayed for him, and probably sang a bit of a song. My sense was that this would be our last visit in this life, and I thanked God profusely for the gift of this unique friendship. It was one of my longest friendships, and though we were not together often, the times of reunion erased the months or years of busy life that intervened.

At his wake and funeral, it struck me that very few of his other friends or family knew about my friendship with this priest who was so important to my response to God's call. His witness gave me a realistic , non-pretentious , and dare I say anything-but naïve insight into priesthood. While I must honestly say that not every priest I have ever come into contact with has inspired me to follow his style of being a priest, Fr. John Kilian was the first to show me what the joy of priesthood can be, not only for the priest himself but the people he serves and loves.

(Un-)Holy Houseguests, Batman!

Movie, TV and comic book heroes have amazingly devoted followers. Fictional characters with super-human powers seem to engage the imagination of audiences and give them some sense that they could actually, even vicariously be super, too. My cynical side often wondered how people who knew Clark Kent could not recognize him without his glasses and suit. Of course, when I wear my contacts and go to the gym people often don't recognize me. (I just wish I didn't have to use a phone booth to change into my workout gear....yeah...right)! Maybe the cape and the spandex, clinging to his super-hero body, were supposed to distract people from saying: "Has anyone ever told you that you sound just like Clark Kent from the Daily Planet?"

Batman's sidekick, Robin, in the TV show that we watched as kids didn't get a whole lot of plot-advancing lines, but often just spouted some exceptional exclamations. What caught my attention was that many of them started with the word "holy." "Holy Hot Dog vendors, Batman! We've gotta catch this evil Dr. Weiner Schnitzel! Let's move our buns!!" Batman and Robin didn't really have superpowers to leap tall buildings or ricochet bullets off their chests, but they had costumes and bat-themed tools to help them climb up the sides of buildings and chase criminals whose homes had very poor architecture: the camera angle was slanted so that you'd know they were "crooked." Brilliant visual punning, I must say!

There was only one day in my life that my family could have called for a super-hero. In neighborhoods like mine in South Buffalo, for generations people knew everyone on their block. They also knew the neighborhood kids, and if they saw any behavior that they knew the parents would want reported, the phone would ring. Or they would step in and offer friendly advice or a pointed reminder that they knew the parents' phone number. As I recall, we left our doors unlocked most of the day, and only put the latch on at night. In our house, that was very practical, with eight people coming and going.

One summer day when I was probably 14 years old or so, we had an uninvited guest come running in our front hall screen door and into our living room. Until that moment this was a typical afternoon for the Quinlivans, with the TV on, Mom out in the kitchen, somebody reading *People* magazine on the couch and my brother Joe wearing stereo headphones, listening to a record and utilizing one of our many rocking chairs.

The unexpected guest was a stranger, who looked very strange, indeed. A young lad in his late teens, he was gasping for breath and hiding behind the door, out of sight from the alleyway. "They're *after* me, man," he said. Mom appeared from the kitchen. "Who's after you?" she asked. "The dudes are after me. I have to hide!" Just at that moment, she noticed that he was holding a knife. He saw her glancing at it, heard her gasp, then ran his finger along its edge and said with a growl "and I know how to **use it**, too!" My sister on the couch held her breath, while Joe kept rocking, completely oblivious and caught up in the music.

Just then, my Dad appeared, coming down the stairs. Without cape or cowl, he stared the guy down and said: "You can't stay here. You have to go, now! Get out of my house," Dad said, firmly. We didn't know if he saw the knife, but the kid was finally not so confident in front of a 6' 2" army veteran defending his family's safety. He ran out the door, and moment later, the police arrived. There had been an unsuccessful robbery of the grocery store two blocks away. Holy *robbin'*, Batman!

The feeling of our home's safety being violated and the awareness of the changing times stayed with us for a while, and from that day the doors were locked almost all the time.

We were grateful that Dad calmly but insistently cleared the house of that intruder. His training as a US Customs inspector came in so handy that day. Ironically, in 1987, when the Federal government decided that inspectors at the border should be armed, my father decided to retire. He had worked almost forty years without a firearm and was not interested in being part of that movement.

It's A Bat, Man!!

If millionaire Bruce Wayne ever shared an attic turned-into-a-bedroom, he might have lost his fascination with bats. My father renovated the third floor of our house into a bedroom for my brother Pat when he became a teen and wanted his own space for concentrating on his homework. When Pat went away to college, Joe and I graduated to the upper room. It was kind of like a loft. Well, really, it was just a renovated attic, and the two of us (who inherited Dad's height) did a lot of ducking, as the slanted ceilings really made standing upright a limited experience in our room. And we have the lumps on our heads to prove it! Either our slanted walls were the underside of the roof, or Batman's villainous enemies lived above us on a fourth floor! Either way, we two "jokers" shared the top level of 205 Stevenson. And while one "egghead" was off to higher education (Sorry, Pat! Batman character references are hard to come by....) the next in line for that room took over.

One pleasant warm Buffalo evening (or should I say on *the* one, warm pleasant Buffalo evening) I had nestled into bed with visions of Marie Osmond dancing in my head (and ice skating, as I recall...) I was awakened by Joe, who had come up to bed later.

"It's a bat," he yelled, as he quickly scrambled down the stairs. I awoke to the sound of something smacking into the walls from side to side. "What do I do?" I cried out, as the remaining family members had soon huddled at the bottom of the stairs. "Don't do anything. Stay where you are!" Easier said than done--- my heart was pounding as I pictured myself trying to escape and seeing a black-winged monster go for my jugular vein. Years later, I wish I had known the lives of the saints in more detail. St. Francis of Assisi once conversed with and befriended a wolf, and St. Martin de Porres had great sympathy for and rapport with rats.

After a few quivering Quinlivan moments under my blanket, I decided to peer out, for the sound of bat wings and battering of walls had ceased. As I looked up, I saw the creature perched atop my lampshade, directly over my head. It was breathing heavily, obviously tired out from its duty as night terrorizer. Okay, to be fair, it probably just wished its sonar radar would find a hole to climb through and get back to its mosquito buffet out in the night.

I decided to make a break for it, slowly dropping a leg off the side of the bed, wrapping myself head-to-toe in the blanket and hurried down the stairs. With one dilemma solved, a new one appeared. Now what do we do?? Dad was not home (probably working a midnight-to-eight shift at the Peace Bridge), so Mom felt that she needed to stir up her "street moxie," a unique gift she had from a scrappy youth in the Depression era. (And, unfortunately, a quality that none of her 6 children inherited)!

She disappeared into her bedroom and came out a moment later with a pair of Dad's boxer shorts on her head. "Bats can get caught in your hair!" she announced like an experienced exterminator. We held it together for a moment, but the sight of our mother in such a get-up was like the home game of I Love Lucy Meets Bat-Fink! Soon, an action plan was formed. One of us found a tennis racket. Mom picked it up like a Wimbledon pro. Somebody remembered that the screen windows of our attic bedroom could easily be removed. If we could get up there and open it, maybe the bat would find its way out without our having to sacrifice it.

A cavalry of batty family members ran up the stairs in a burst of courage. They turned on a light---bats are blind, we figured, but we can use the lamp! In a rush of swinging tennis rackets and shouts of "get out" that would have surely petrified our front hall robber-visitor, somehow the bat got hit. It landed on the floor in the storage area next to our room and a brave soldier dropped our wrought iron antique Christmas tree base on it. The creature was stilled. But, having the decorative tree base lifted, the bat then made a buzzing sound and came back to life. We all ran down the stairs in a flurry and slammed the door. We ended up leaving the window open all night, and sleeping on the couches. And man, we never saw that bat again. Holy hilarity, Batman!

Chapter Two

I DON'T WANT YOUR PITY. I WANT YOUR DONUT!

In the Scriptures, the Book of Ecclesiastes 3, verse 1-15 lists "a time to plant and a time to uproot the plant...." and a long list of "times" concluding with "God has placed the timeless in their hearts, without men's ever discovering...the work that God has done."

For much of my young adult life, I felt as though I could not make any headway with my hopes, dreams and life plans. After high school, I toyed with the idea of becoming an actor and or singer for a living. But God had other plans. A case of acute strep throat kept me from participating in a live version of TV's wacky "Gong Show." I auditioned for and was accepted into the talent competition at the Niagara Falls Convention Center that had everyone thinking they could be discovered... but would end up being a chance for the judges to mock every participant mercilessly. It wasn't really a talent search as much as target practice, and I dodged that bullet by losing my voice through the blessing of an infection.

For the audition for the Gong Show, I avoided the *Battle Hymn of the Republic* and instead decided to sing a song I really loved. In my continuing stream of naiveté, I chose

Tomorrow from the Broadway musical, *Annie.* I loved the tune, and the words were easy enough to do…and, in the right key, I could do it justice and hold the long last note while (in my imagination) the throngs of people would jump to their feet, unable to hold their wild cheers. In hindsight, I now thank God for strep throat! I realize that He saved me from all kinds of jokes about judges wanting to pluck out my eyes like the cartoon orphan or asking who the surgeon was who made me "Orphan Andy" or some sarcastic snip telling me my song made them wish it *was* tomorrow so that they could forget my performance today.

My mother used to regale us with her stories of signing up for Miss Jane Keeler's Drama School in her early twenties. The lady in charge was an old-school stage diva, who wished to share her vast knowledge from years as an actress on Buffalo's stages with neophytes who would pay tuition. For a very brief time, after high school, I attended the next generation of Miss Keeler's work, the Studio Arena Theater School. Thinking I could somehow find and hone a stage career that would make my high school directors realize that they had overlooked me, I paid thirty dollars tuition and took a Metro bus to downtown Buffalo one evening.

The world of theater was very different from my school plays. I only participated in three sessions, finding more joy in coming home to share stories with the family of how fish-out-of-water I felt. One memorable exercise in acting class instructed us to pair off, and one at a time, we were to become a mound of formless clay. (I had seen some pretty sluggish and lifeless people in high school on Monday mornings… and had been one myself at times)! I cannot recall what the young woman who molded me was trying to make, but I somehow recall that I had her kneeling, with her hands folded, posing as St. Bernadette in the Lourdes grotto. Needless to say, the other students and teacher were hardly enthusiastic about my creative work as a theatrical artist with a religious twist. I decided, too, that I was better off lighting a candle in front of statues of saints than molding them from wanna-be actresses!

The Summer before my freshman year at Buffalo State, I was hired at Mercy Hospital, which was about eight blocks from my house. All through my college years, I worked part-time as a Medical Record File Clerk. (Not exactly fascinating work.) You had to pick up a chart, read its file number and then put it in the folder with the corresponding number on it. It's what you have to call mundane work, very repetitive and even more dull after the first ten minutes. What saved me was the office's staff of ladies. I was the only male employee in the Medical Record room; fairly healthy (for someone who took every opportunity to avoid gym class) and able to carry heavy items for the ladies. I served a purpose of sorts. I was also still a "growing boy" and enjoyed the many birthday coffee breaks with donuts or cake. The hospital cafeteria had awesome fresh donuts each day, which explains why I was also growing horizontally much of the time!

There are still scars on my hands from renegade staples that refused to lie flat when slammed into the pile of pages. Paper-cuts were a constant risk, and my Irish skin proved a canvas for the tiny, nearly-invisibly but highly painful lacerations. Hazard of the filing trade, it seems. Yet never a serious enough injury to have applied for Workman's Compensation. My main duty of filing consisted of keeping an eye on a designated shelf where charts were piled high. As soon as a morning's worth of filing was complete, charts awaiting physician signatures would be piled up again. It was something akin to shoveling snow in Buffalo on a January day. Occasionally, there would be a sense of the importance of my little job. A call from the Emergency Room, Cardiac Care, Intensive Care or Maternity would come for a specific patient's medical record. I could race to find and pull the file, and get it to the department where a doctor was waiting to study it before deciding on the care of a patient.

So, apparently I underestimate this work as simply filing. It would be wrong to glamorize it in any way, but the other part of being a file clerk was retrieving files. Doctors would be doing a research study and requisition a number of charts, sometimes one hundred or so. They would drop off a request with a deadline. This was good training for later in life, when phone messages pile up on the rectory phone, and requests for answers to pastoral questions appear from every direction.

For about nine years, I filed. And I re-filed, and I carried boxes to and fro. But for the gift of multi-tasking mentally, I would have been bored to death. My imagination worked overtime, and ideas for writing projects would break through the boredom. In the office, I ended up becoming responsible for our Christmas parties, voluntarily ran gambling pools for World Series, Super Bowls, Kentucky Derby and other Catholic traditions. Oh…sorry, this kind of gambling is an Irish tradition. It would be inappropriate to have run Bingo games during the work day. Even though it's commonly acknowledged that Bingo, for many years, was like an eighth sacrament in most Catholic parishes!

After graduating from Buffalo State College with my Bachelor's degree in Journalism, Broadcasting and Speech (I had decided that working behind the cameras, writing and producing could also be more fun than acting) I found the job market in Buffalo completely non-cooperative. My boss, Sr. Mary Kenneth Mullen, kindly created a full-time position for me, as I expected to be hired away soon after graduation. However, several years after graduating, I could sense that my friends in the office were often saying "Poor Bill. He just can't get a job in his field!"

What I learned in working with an office of all women, with a vowed religious as the boss, ladies my mother's age and a number closer to my own age, was invaluable insight into the female species. As the minority at the coffee break and lunch table, I was subjected to endless conversations about the dating lives of the single ladies. Then, because I worked there so long, the engagements, wedding showers, weddings, baby showers, and so on. It was really a great gift to go through the seasons of one another's lives, even the difficult times in the death of family members. After my ordination, I ended up doing Baptisms, funerals and other kinds of ministry to these same friends.

The one area where it seemed that I might have been given too much information was during their pregnancies. I would hear every detail from sonogram to the final push of labor and delivery. As a child's birth was nearing, I was always excited for my co-workers and their husbands. But I had to tell them that the only men who need to know so many details of childbirth are the fathers of the children and the obstetrician, if the doctor is a male. On the other hand, I got pretty good at not blushing when they'd ask a late-term mother "How many centimeters are you dilated?" while I bit into my jelly donut. I'd tell myself that someday I might get stuck in the hospital elevator with a woman in labor, and be able to tap into my rich treasury of information should I ever have to coach someone through the birthing process.

While office life was mostly a joy, and I adjusted to discussions of biological clocks, my vocational compass was still on pause. Poor Bill was getting older, and more than a little desperate, so I told myself that maybe relocation was the answer. New York City, Los Angeles... why not?? Well, I found out rather quickly why not. Embarking on a few "job hunting" expeditions, I was aghast at the reality of how many people had my same dream, how many thousands were vying for a few job openings, and the harsh reality that employers weren't about to offer one of them to "Poor Bill," who had no experience in the field. I couldn't even find a job listing for file clerks at Hollywood studios or New York television network offices.

A lucky break came when a co-worker's husband told me about a part-time position at a local FM radio station. He was an on-air personality there and could get me an interview. Miraculously, I was interviewed, then offered a part-time job writing news, weather and sports (Sports?!? *Nothing* is impossible with God)! While it was only 3 hours per day and could hardly finance my used car for more than a week's worth of gas, it was the chance that I had hoped and prayed for. Four years out of college, with a Bachelor's degree and nothing much to show for it besides paper cuts and the knowledge of when to tell a birthing mother to "push," and visiting the hospital chapel regularly to beg God for what I thought I wanted, opportunity knocked.

Through all those years, people from my parish would regularly ask if I was still interested in becoming a priest. People often ask young men who are involved in parish life whether they have heard God calling them to priesthood. From about the age of eleven until half-way through high school, the answer was yes. I was thinking about it. My social life revolved around church activities, I couldn't seem to get enough of the holy stuff. But when the show-biz bug bit, and it seemed that the spotlight was calling (or was it *another* light???) I concluded that I had somehow gotten caught up in the enthusiasm of my friend Fr. Ray's calling. But even after he was away at seminary, people always kept asking. Even people who hardly knew me would say "Have you ever considered being a priest?" And it actually began to annoy me. It felt like pressure from the outside when my heart had decided that I had a plan that would surely bring me the life I now desired.

Instead of snapping at people, my defense was to turn to humor. One of my well-rehearsed answers was "I can't get up that early!" But then, when I got hired by WJYE-FM to write the news for the morning drive show, and they told me I'd have to be there by 5:00 AM, I rationalized that to achieve your dreams, you've got to sacrifice. A few months later, when the question of priesthood was again raised, I reached for my need-for-sleep excuse and it no longer worked. Then I realized that my priest friend was still sleeping while I was up at 4:00 in the morning, racing downtown, writing traffic reports and re-writing stories from the news wire machine which chugged out newsprint constantly.

The format of the radio station when I started was the kind of music older people listened to. It was a mostly instrumental type of fare, Mantovani and an orchestra called 101 Strings. Elevator music, really. And at twenty-four years old, I needed something with more of a beat to help me stay awake. So I would turn down the over-head speakers at my desk and play a pop music station while I typed out the news. Thankfully, a format change arrived soon after I did and it became a soft rock station. It was much of the music I had in my LP collection, Carpenters, Anne Murray, etc. You know, the head-banger stuff....not! But it was so much more contemporary, that now the only reason I listened to other stations in the back office was to "borrow" traffic information. Our station never had a traffic copter, so I was instructed to keep an ear on one of the AM stations that had one. Once a tie- up or fender-bender was reported, it was pubic information, so we didn't consider it stealing. I tried to talk the announcer into drumming on his ribs to sound as though he were in a helicopter. He chose not to.

I learned to love coffee with tremendous devotion in that year of dragging myself out of bed before the birds awoke. While I was temporarily impressed with finally being in a field closer to my education, I had to keep my hospital job. After working in the "radio business" for those few hours, I'd jump in my car and go to Mercy Hospital for my 8-hour shift. I found that the glamour of working in the media world wore off very fast. But it was insulation against considering myself "Poor Bill." It just made me "Dead-Tired Bill." Was this happiness, I wondered and kept praying for the bigger miracle of a full-time position in my field of study. But the Lord had lessons to teach me before that would happen.

When my first anniversary of writing news for the morning show was coming up, the station hired a media consultant to evaluate the morning show. Their professional opinion was that Joe Chille, the announcer, should be joined by an on-air news person not only to read the news but also to chat in between songs. That was the trend in the mid-1980's, but then, so too, were the garish sweaters Bill Cosby wore, and thankfully fashion trends wear out faster than sweaters that look like a yarn factory barfed on them. The station asked me to do an audition tape, saying that they really wanted me for the job. Thankful that for this audition I didn't have to sing *Battle Hymn of the Republic* or risk being gonged in front of thousands of strangers, I went against my gut and agreed to try it. But something in me was very wary, and I put off the idea and tried to bow out of the job altogether, gracefully. My sense was that the radio microphone and my nasal South Buffalo accent were not a compatible match. And my confidence at that point was firmly entrenched behind the scenes.

They persisted, so I worked with the overnight deejay one morning on a tape (yes…a cassette tape…this was during what now looks like a technological Stone Age). I'm a rather soft-spoken guy, as my father was. So Sal Paonessa, a larger-than-life radio vet said to me "You gotta read each story like it's the most important thing you'll say all day. With passion, with gusto!!" He suggested I kind of belt it out like Neil Diamond singing the first line of his hit song *Love On The Rocks*. Try as I might, I was used to simply reading and not terribly convincing. The station relieved me of my duties as well as my anxiety at having to wear headphones and listen to my own voice every morning.

I knew that reading news on the radio was not my gift, my calling. And later, I would find my way to proclaiming the Good News, with as much passion as a soft-spoken Irishman can conjure! I realize now that I couldn't "sell" the news because I didn't have any passion for it. I now have a lead role in the liturgy, and even enjoy the singing parts. Because it's not a talent show or radio show, not about me, really, but the One worth believing in, serving and even dying for. And I know that my current boss would never call me "Poor Bill." He knew that when I discovered the real purpose of my life, I'd be more rich than the people in New York and Los Angeles I once had hoped desperately to impress.

But years before that happened, I'd continue to wander. My sense that I had not found the niche in entertainment was a nagging reality, so I started to respond to Want Ads in fields of advertising and marketing. I'd decided that I had to change my dream if there was a job opening where I thought someone might hire me. My cousin Rocky Molloy had a print shop in South Buffalo. He would re-print my resume for me—free—every time I changed my focus. I used to say that my resume saw more printings than the Gideon bible! Admittedly, some versions of my resume had exaggerations of the truth that the Bible's commandment against lying might disagree with, strongly. The experience that suited me to apply for a marketing position was really selling Easter candy, Christmas cards and yearbook sponsors at Catholic schools. With the right spin it was "extensive sales experience with management potential."

Reading the Sunday Want Ads can become a very depressing experience. Every company wants a self-starter. Who's ever going to admit that they need jumper cables to get them motivated to do dead-end work? Many of the employers were not really honest, either. If they wanted talented, professional applicants for entry-level jobs, I often wondered why they didn't just use the alumni offices of all the local colleges to contact recent graduates. One of my worst interviews was at a coffee shop. I had responded to an ad for a marketing position at a "fast-growing local communications business." My resume actually brought a phone call, where a man arranged to meet me for coffee to do an interview. After an hour of his side-stepping my questions, he flipped over the paper placemat and drew an umbrella, and revealed the name of a national chain of door-to-door cleaning products. I was duped, and quickly excused myself, leaving him to pay the bill and hopefully use some of his great cleaning products on the booth's stained counter-top.

There was only one more lame attempt to break into show business. Robert Redford was coming to Buffalo to shoot "The Natural," and my friend Mike Carabelli and I quickly signed up to be extras. It paid about $ 30 per day, and we even got fitted for costumes. Somewhere there's a photo of me in a navy blue pinstriped zoot suit wearing a fedora. I was probably about twenty-two, but looked like a fifteen year old trying on his Dad's clothes! The movie's baseball scenes were shot at Buffalo's old Bisons stadium nicknamed The Rockpile. The name said it all---not glamorous, but rather historic.

One day, they gave me a costume as a hospital orderly. Actually, there were about a dozen of us, women in nurse outfits and guys dressed as 1940s-style hospital staff. I loved the irony...I had taken a day off from my job at a hospital to play a hospital worker, so I could get to Hollywood and leave the hospital. Circular reasoning? Unrealistic? Sure! But it was fun trying. My day as an orderly actually took place on location at the Buffalo Psychiatric Hospital, one block South of my alma mater Buffalo State College. The irony of a Hollywood production company and a gaggle of wanna-be actors at such a facility was truly priceless!

We ended up standing around all day in costume, sequestered down the hall and behind a door from where

Glenn Close and Redford were shooting a hospital scene. At one point, outside the building, I had a Glenn Close encounter of a casual kind; I said hello and she smiled and returned the greeting. But the rest of the day, I prayed and hoped that there would be a call for a six-foot orderly with pasty Irish skin. No such call came. When the day of shooting ended, I handed back my costume and went home.

In my convoluted fantasy of becoming famous, on the days when we were filling seats in the stadium for crowd reaction shots, I harkened back to my role as a baseball player in the chorus of "Damn Yankees" in high school. (Which I mostly called Darned Yankees unless I was with other cast members. Such language seemed inappropriate for a young Catholic gentleman. But, for the good of the show....I made damn, I mean darn sure I was accurate!) I watched to see if any of the ballplayers got hurt, and was ready to step in. What didn't occur to me was that the musical experience would translate very little to actual, even movie-fake baseball!!

I finally took a full-time job as a portrait photographer for a national chain of photo studios. It got me out of my file clerk position, but I soon realized that this was another dead end. The promised salary was hidden in the phrase "could be as much as…" instead of a definite figure. After giving my notice at the hospital and saying goodbye to file clerk purgatory and my long-time friends, I found myself in another fine employment mess, for less than I was making at the prior position. I went through their photography training, but quit that job after one year, realizing that the manager was lying to his employees. I have always been naïve…but I'm not stupid.

Writing radio news was great creative training for later in life where morning Mass homilies are better if they're brief. But this photography business was more of a cut-throat competitive, almost sleazy-behind-the-scenes deal, and it was not a good fit for me. (Worse than the zoot suit in *The*

Natural!) The lie I un-covered involved our appointment secretaries in another location who would tell me that I had appointments with a number of clients at various times. I would anticipate their arrival, and end up sitting for hours since no one came in. Then, at peak times like Saturday morning and afternoon, they would actually schedule three to five portrait sittings in a fifteen minute time period. One could be a three month-old infant, another would be a group of six adults, and a third could be a collection of cousins under the age of four, with the combined attention span of a gnat with a sinus headache. Customers would flood the waiting room, getting more and more annoyed that I was running behind. No matter how fast I set up the baby chair, squeaked the toy, did my best Kermit the Frog voice on speed and attempted witty statements to make adults smile, I always ended up feeling like I was stuck in Los Angeles rush hour traffic and every honking horn was aimed at me!

My year as a photographer was some fun, because I enjoyed the challenge of trying to get people to smile or laugh. I got pretty good at coaxing smiles from babies, toddlers and even teens. But pet sittings were hardest. Great Danes won't smile on command, and the nature of pit bulls is only to show their teeth in connection to negative emotions. But I also discovered that German Shepherds just don't care for the Irish. Come to think of it, the Setters were easier, and even Schnauzers responded more pleasantly than some one-year-olds who needed a nap instead of a photo session at 2:00 PM, or a diaper change, immediately!

At one point in my late twenties, I was unemployed for six months, so I took a position at an office temporary agency. It was work, but it was worse than being a full-time file clerk. No donuts... and they could send you anywhere, to do the most dreary tasks. If a local bank was doing a huge mailing, I'd get sent to an office building in downtown Buffalo and stuff envelopes for 8 hours. At one point, I was a messenger for a law firm and carried legal documents from the office to the courthouse. Exciting? No! And not at all what I kept praying for!

I now see it all as an elaborate lesson in humility and patience. And without my faith and sense of humor, I don't know where I would have ended up. The humor ended up being very helpful to keep me sane…or at least make a dash toward sanity. When I was feeling eternally stuck in the filing job, the person who micro-filmed the charts would show me some very cute or downright hilarious photos of newborn babies. At the time, the photos were discarded when the charts were being stored on microfilm, because they didn't come out well on film. It isn't really fair to stick a baby in front of a camera two minutes after their first breath. It's surprising that their first words aren't Mama and Pappa-razzi.

At one point, I asked my friend Debbie to save them for me. I would sort through them, looking for expressions I could caption. Of course, before using them, I'd cut off the name, respecting confidentiality. I'd include a silly captioned photo in friends' birthday cards, calling my new product a Baby-Gram. Once, the Buffalo News listed a job opening for an Advertising Copyrighter, I made a one-page storyboard of funny looking babies with captions. Each baby would explain why Bill Quinlivan was a good choice for this job (and, of course, one tyke was shoving his fist in his mouth so I wrote: "Do you serve donuts on coffee breaks??") The Baby-Grams were a hit, and got me an interview….but not the job. They told me they just had to meet the person crazy enough to send this with a resume. A few days later, they sent me what could have been called a Reject-o-Gram.

The low point in all my job hunting had to be rejection by the Golden Arches. All my friends could get jobs there, and I had 5 years of Bingo kitchen expertise. But I was rejected by *the* Ronald McDonald! Adding insult to injury, a sibling noted that I might have applied for the Ronald role since my feet would fit the clown shoes. At the time, I had no clue that I'd be eventually be working for the King of Kings instead of the king of burgers.

A New Kind of Filing: Taxes!

As the humor of Heaven would have it, I eventually found a position with the Internal Revenue Service. My parents had always insisted that civil service jobs are steady, and the pay and benefits were pretty good. After all, Dad worked for the government as a US Customs Inspector most of his adult life and supported eight people on that one income.

I was as ill-suited for that kind of work as I would be training camels to jump through the eye of a needle. Finance has never been my strength, mathematics was on my "avoid like the plague" list right after gym class. But they hired me to work in the Taxpayer Service division along with about two hundred others at the same time. As entry-level employees, we were really only supposed to greet the caller, assess their questions and answer only the simplest inquiry like "If I live in Brooklyn, where do I mail my forms?"

Much of what we had to do on the phone was competently say "I'm not trained in that area of taxation. Please hold while I transfer you to someone who can help you!" But another large chunk of our energy was simply trying to calm people down so we could reason with them. Any letter from the Internal Revenue service is usually greeted by the average citizen as a frightful piece of mail. If the government is sending me a letter, they surmise, it MUST be bad news! And very often, the letter might only raise a question regarding the prior year's tax form.

As a priest, I rely often on skills that I gained at the IRS. Unfortunately, I cannot easily use the line they taught us "I'm not trained in that area…let me transfer you to someone who can help you." Parishioners at the church door on Sunday don't like that response! Besides, sometimes I'm the person someone else transferred their call to; so I have to be ready to calm them if possible. Without taxing them, or my patience, too much.

One day while on duty at the IRS, my supervisor came around the corner from his cubicle and said, with a smile: "Quinlivan—I have a good test for you. I just put this lady on hold…she's ballistic. Let me see how you handle her." One of the more disconcerting elements of on-the-phone taxpayer work is that your supervisors monitor your calls. They can even, with a beeping noise, interrupt you…if they hear you're giving the wrong answer. I'm awfully glad the Lord doesn't do that in the Confessional. I'd be SO embarrassed!!

It was an elderly lady, so I took the call, and I recognized her frightened, panic tone. I found myself getting more calm as the call went on. When she sensed that I was trying to help, she got a bit calmer. I followed the directives of my training, asking: "Do you have the letter in front of you? Can you please read me the first line?" She did…and the first sentence said "This is not a bill." So I said "See-it's not a bill. I wouldn't lie to you….etc."

Afterwards, the supervisor came back around the corner and told me he thought that I handled it better than he could. Wow—I wondered: is there a donut that comes with this pat on the back? A pat on the back was really enough, though, as I realized that people in a tizzy often just need someone to listen. I think that I had to transfer her again, but she was thanking me instead of cursing the IRS. And I was thanking God!!

From Joan to Jesus

A bright light that appeared like the star of Bethlehem over my search for "a life," as we say, came in a most unusual way. I was working at the hospital filing, and writing radio news in the early, early morning while most priests were still sleeping, and I bought a resource book for people who want to write for TV, movies, and such called *The Writer's Market*. It contains hundreds of addresses and phone numbers for agents, producers and production companies to contact with your script or idea. At that time, I had written a script for a TV movie-of-the-week and wanted to mail it out to Hollywood so they could beg to produce it, offer me a contract and send advance payment for my work. At the time, one script would pay more than I made in any year since I started working.

Well, the begging continued to be on my end. I was writing at night while working two jobs during the day. Then, while flipping through the small telephone-book size *Writer's Market*, I came across a very brief section entitled "Gag Writing." At first I thought... "My gosh, what would you write when you're vomiting? That's disgusting!" Then it dawned on me that it was comedy writing, gags. Chuckles instead of up-chuck. What a relief!

Humor seems to come rather naturally to some people. Certain friends, neighbors, or co-workers might encourage a person they consider funny to do a riff on a topic they enjoy joking about. But it was sort of bizarre trying to think funny for the sake of selling a joke. It's much easier to surprise people than sit down and write humor. People who don't appreciate your humor will bark: "What, are you a COMEDIAN?" as if it's one of the worst professions in the world. Actually, I've always highly admired comics. While I had known that I could sometimes make my family laugh (or...groan at my puns), these professionals stood up in front of audiences, took the risk that their material might fall flat. To me, that's a kind of courage most of us don't possess.

So as I paged through the Gag Writing section, I suddenly stopped at the listing that said Joan Rivers Productions. I had enjoyed her humor for years, and was rather shocked that she paid writers. That sense was instantly replaced with the thought: I wonder if Joan Rivers would buy a joke from me?? If not, I could at least brag that I was rejected by both Ronald McDonald and one of my favorite comics. So I wrote for the submission forms, and while I waited for a response I started thinking like Joan Rivers while I was filing medical records. It was actually a strange but enjoyable way to pass the time as I bandaged my paper cuts, heard the latest chat on who was pregnant in the office, and filed away.

After I mailed in the first batch of one-liners, my thought was "Even if I never hear from her, just to think she might have read my jokes is thrilling." Then, about three weeks later on a warm July day in 1984, my self-addressed, stamped envelope came back with the news that she was buying two jokes. I was completely shocked. And, as I knew in advance, the going rate for one-liners was ten dollars. Running around the house with the letter in my hand, I told everyone in the family. At the time, Joan was Johnny Carson's permanent guest host on the Tonight Show and was very popular. So I signed the form and mailed it back, and waited for my check.

I then started keeping vigil at the corner drug store waiting for the TV Guide to arrive, and praying that Carson would soon have a vacation week. And it happened about three weeks later. I set the VCR to record every night, and watched breathlessly. (For readers under twenty-one, before digital technology there was tape. We recorded TV shows and music on it. Okay, go back to your modern gadgets now!)

On Thursday night, during the monologue, she suddenly turned to a topic I had included in my joke submissions:

Yoko Ono. After a scene-setting favorite line about buying Yoko's greatest hits album and finding nothing inside, she told MY JOKE, and the audience laughed. Surreal is the only word I can use to describe it. Me, the guy who couldn't figure out what to do with his life...my joke was told on network TV. ("You know how Yoko has those sunglasses that cover half her face? She could use TWO pairs!!") Over the next several years, I hit pay-dirt several more times. In fact, every time I sent a batch of jokes she bought a few, the second time it was three, then five and one time she purchased six. Ironically, the last batch I sent was right before I entered priestly formation. That was the only time I never heard back. It was okay, I had finally found my calling. And ironically, for the first seventeen years I ministered as a priest, the stipend for a Mass was...ten dollars. And I have to say, it's even more thrilling to be able to say Mass than write comedy professionally!

Backstage in Buffalo

I've only met Joan Rivers once. I'd met and enjoyed her signature on checks from her office, but never met her. In my second-last year of seminary, she was booked to play the awesome Shea's Buffalo Theater, a true gem in our city's theater district. In fact, in my unemployed days I was a volunteer usher there and got to see a lot of great shows for free. Anyway, I got tickets, and the day of the show I called the theater and told them I had written gags for Joan but never met her. I asked if she was going to do a "meet and greet" (as they call it in show business...and as I sometimes call it now when the Bishop stays after Confirmation!)

It had to be the hand of God, because the young woman who answered the phone gave me the name of the stage manager and it was someone I knew from my TV Production classes at college. Her name was Joy--a great word to describe my feelings at that news. They instructed me to write a letter to Miss Rivers and tell her my story of why I wanted to come backstage. I was to leave the envelope at the Shea's box office for Joy before the show.

We arrived very early at the theater and a short while after we were seated; an announcement came over the sound system "Would Bill Gilvengin please come to the box office. Miss Rivers would like to see you after the show." I turned to my sister Mary and said "They did NOT say Quinlivan.... but let's go.... tonight I'm Bill... whoever-they-said. If anybody's going backstage it's me!" I hurried to the box office and claimed to be the person they were looking for. They gave instructions where to go afterwards.

All during the show, I was getting more nervous and excited. I can hardly remember much about it except that she didn't tell any of MY jokes that night. And she was picking on Marie Osmond, which, to me, after Julie Andrews was a person to whom I had a lifelong fan-attachment. (Several years later, Marie toured in Sound of Music and I saw her in it at Shea's Buffalo. Talk about mixed metaphors. She hasn't ask to meet me. ...yet.)

Mary and I were taken backstage and Joan Rivers came walking in carrying her Yorkshire Terrier, Spike. There were other people infringing on my Joan Rivers moment, but I waited patiently and then awkwardly introduced myself. I told her that I had written one-liners for her through the mail, and I was thrilled to meet her. Then I told her that I was in seminary and hoped to be a Catholic priest in about 3 years. She surprised me: "Great! Good for you. Let me know when you graduate!" A few of the backstage interlopers had their moments, and posed for pictures. Mary and I did, too. Again, Joan turned to me and said "Let me know when you graduate." Then when we said goodbye she stood as high as a little lady can to shout over the crowd 'don't forget. Let me know when you graduate!"

I remembered from reading in one of her books that after her husband Edgar Rosenburg tragically took his own life, she called for a Catholic priest. That always seemed to indicate her respect for the clergy. For a woman who made a living being professionally disrespectful, the offstage Joan was really a sweet lady.

In early 1994 when I was studying my fool head off for Comprehensive Theological Exams in my last semester at Christ the King Seminary, an off-hand remark by one of my classmates "You would never sell THAT line to Joan Rivers…" reminded me of the repeated request to know about my graduation. So, although for me the graduation was nowhere near as important at my ordination, I sent a letter to Joan Rivers Productions in L.A. and got back to studying. In May, the morning of graduation, a telegram came from Joan Rivers. It congratulated me on my hard work…and she wasn't joking! Now I guess that I'm probably the only priest in the history of our diocese to receive a telegram from one of the world's best-loved comics.

If people say 'What are you--- a comedian??" I now say: "No---but I used to write for one!"

Chapter Three

WHAT IS YOUR SONG?

When I was a seminarian, I joined the choir. It seemed a natural, comfortable move. I'm not sure if other people experience this, but there's usually music of some sort playing in my head. Sometimes, it's a song I love, at other times, a song I don't particularly care for, but it somehow gets lodged in there, as if someone pressed a repeat button without asking my opinion. It's possible to change that channel, but there's no remote control device that can hit pause. Is it me-- am I what they call a radio-head?

From 6th grade onward, I always participated in school and parish choirs. There's something so affirming to be part of a group of people whose voices blend, to make a musical sound so much bigger than one voice can accomplish. I also grew up in a house filled with music, and when the Quinlivan kids weren't singing in the school St. Patrick's Day show we were taking turns plugging the headphones into our stereo.

The song we became known for belting out each March on the stage at St. Teresa's was taught to us by our father, a folk song that I've never heard anywhere else. The cute factor was high when we inserted the family name. The crowd loved it... at least, we were told they did!

What Is Your Song?

తతతతతతత

What is your song?
Have you quieted your heart to listen for a tune?
Life gets too long without an inspiration
and a melody to croon.
If every breath is a gift,
that we can give back to the Lord
then, wrap it in a joyful noise;
they'll say that your eagle's soared
no matter the cacophony of sounds out-poured.

O, when father papered the parlor, sure, you couldn't see father for paste,
He was dabbin' it here and dabbin' it there, paste and paper everywhere,
Mother was stuck to the ceiling and the kids were stuck to the floor
You never saw the Quinlivan family so stuck up before!

There's something so rich and sweet about singing with your family. I've always liked musical families and brother and sister acts because the voices blend like butter into frosting! The timbre of the voices is so similar, and it reminds me of the sound you can get in a recording studio when you add background vocals or harmonies with your own voice. I often joke when I sing with my pre-recorded tracks that include those vocals that I'm "beside myself." While the Quinlivan family may never be found in the music stores alongside the Andrews Sisters, Everly Brothers or even the von Trapp Family singers, we have our memories of those days on stage.

We didn't have many male voices in our church choir at St. Teresa's, so I would attempt to sing a tenor or bass part, thought I am actually more comfortable as a baritone. But in that situation, it's something akin to musical pinch-hitting-- with an occasional balk. Some notes I just had not the courage to swing at! Seminary choir was different. For our weekly Masses, it was all men. We were directed by a religious woman, but week in and week out we were without alto or soprano voices. Though the second tenors would occasionally take teasing that they were on the brink.

There were opportunities for seminarians to cantor, to lead the hymns and sometimes sing the verses of the psalm response and Gospel acclamation. But my insecurity kept me from stepping up to sing solo. Besides, there seemed to already be a number of seminarians with great voices. And as I had never been really singled out for solos in school musicals or "folk group" in the 1970's, I figured I was a choral singer, a team player. I just loved making music, so that was fine with me. For a time…

When I would go to the campus gym at night to shoot baskets (yes, I eventually out-grew my gym-o-phobia!) I would cool down before I went back to my room by walking laps. As I can only get excited about exercise by listening to music, I'd carry to the gym what we used to call a "boom box"—a portable tape and, later, CD player. Truth be told, I'd almost always turn off the lights in the gym, blast the music and dance for exercise. Shooting baskets was dull after only a few minutes. Dance was always my favorite form of a workout, because it could let me be literally moved by the music instead of counting repetitions of lifting weights or checking my pulse in aerobics classes.

Singing in such a sizeable hall with echo actually provided great reverberation, or "reverb" as they call it in the recording trade. So when I sang, and heard back the echo, I realized that this sounded okay. It took me two full years to get the courage together to become a cantor, and in the meantime, God nudged me onward as I watched the best singing upper classmen graduate and fewer music ministers arrive in the classes behind mine. Once I started cantoring, I found it profoundly satisfying. The approach of stage performance, with the expectation of applause was taken away, as the appropriate response to sung prayer is to pray more deeply, not to clap.

Are There Songs in Me??

The longer I loved music, the more I came to realize the difference between various kinds of singing as a technical talent/skill and the more personal, heart-connected music making that involves your soul. For decades, I have been a devoted fan of Amy Grant. Even to this day, certain songs of hers just strike me as such deep expressions of her spirit that I feel as though I know her. It's no stretch to imagine myself, should we ever meet, quoting her lyrics back to her until she feels just a little uncomfortable with my access to her songs in my head. (Though I can hardly remember the combination to my gym locker, and always say my memory is like an Etch-A-Sketch, and if I turn my head too fast everything gets erased).

One evening in the late 1990's, my friend Fred Caserta, the founder of Buffalo's Kingdom Bound Christian Music Festival invited me to come to their prayer group and bring my guitar because their regular musician was not available. By this time, I had been playing with a Buffalo-based music ministry called Voices of Mercy for several years, and knew quite a few contemporary "praise and worship" songs. Of course, by "knew", I mean that with written lyrics and chords in front of me, I could play and sing melodies and match tempos. Memorization of even my own compositions remains an Impossible Dream for my mind! And my most-accessible nightmare: being asked, spontaneously, to sing *Memory* from the musical Cats…and in the heights of irony, getting about half a sentence in and forgetting the words completely…. I would instantly go into the Mister Rogers Neighborhood language of the kitty puppet that spoke only one word, repeatedly: "Meow, meow, meow meow… all alone in the meow meow…."

The night of the Kingdom Bound Ministries prayer group gathering, after we finished about an hour of singing and praising the Lord, one of the women whom I had just met that evening approached me. She asked if I was writing my own songs. At that point, I had co-written only one song with three other people. I'd characterize my contribution as rhyme consultant at best. This woman, whose name has disappeared in my shaken Etch-A-Sketch years ago, told me that she had a vision of me during the prayer and praise:

"I saw you sitting with pen and paper---a golden pen. As you wrote, I saw musical notes flowing out of the pen and swirling up into the air." Then she paused. "It seems to me

41

that the Lord wants you to write songs." I thanked her politely for sharing this, and somewhere inside me my response was... "Songs? You want ME to write songs?? Well...you're gonna have to help me Lord!" And I have to say, in time, He has. And I've discovered that unique sense of favorite music not just being "your song," which you relate to in a special moment where it personally touched you. Though it's taken me years to get used to even trying to say it, I can now call some of the tunes I sing "my songs."

Everybody has a story to tell, a life to live, and I have come to believe, a "song" to sing. Even those who cannot match a pitch or whose own mothers would say, upon hearing an attempt to sing "Maybe painting is your gift", has a song in them. It's not even necessarily music to anyone else's ears but rather to God Himself. But it is your song. Finding that song, recognizing our calling and giftedness, is one of my passions in working for the Church. Having found mine, I can witness to others that if you keep searching, you'll find it.

Creating songs has come about for me in a variety of ways. An idea pops into my head, and I rush to write it down (on paper, NOT the Etch-A-Sketch....who can turn those little white knobs that fast anyway)? Often when I spend time in Eucharistic Adoration, ideas for lyrics are born and written into my prayer journals. Sometimes those same words sit there for several months or years, remaining poetry until an occasion comes to put a tune to it. Other times, however, there's a quicker musical birth. I rather enjoy the adventure of watching and waiting, and the often-surprising results, so that I feel more like a passenger and participant on the journey than navigator or captain. The Lord is my songwriting captain. It's His lifeboats that I want!

On Holy Trinity Sunday one year, I was invited to celebrate early morning Mass for the cloistered Dominican Sisters in Buffalo when their chaplain was away. That same day, I was scheduled to have Mass at St. Luke's Mission about

2 hours later. Because the two places are only about a six minute drive apart and my rectory was about thirty minutes away, rather than drive home and back, I decided to stay in the beautiful chapel of the sisters and pray a while. The silence in the stone-built monastery is perhaps the most dependably available silence anywhere in the diocese of Buffalo. It's a delightful prayer respite from parish churches on Sunday with the sounds that often distract a person seeking to pray.

Pondering the mystery of God as three persons in one, I realized that my adoration of the Blessed Sacrament usually focused on the divine person Jesus, and I became more aware that the Heavenly Father and Holy Spirit were also oh-so-worthy of praise. I opened my journal and sat, simply soaked in silence for a significant period of time, and then began to write what would become "Be Adored," a hymn for this great feast day. The out-pouring of ideas onto the page in an orderly manner doesn't always (or hardly ever!) happen in my writing, but the verses flowed, one after another, the rhymes come easily and the first draft was virtually the finished product. I could even hear a melody in my head as I was writing. When it was recorded, it would have been fitting to give co-writing credit in the CD liner notes to the angels in prayer with me that morning! But where would one send the royalty check?

Another time, my heart was heavy with the pain and confusion of what felt like constant news reports that priests were being removed from their ministry due to horrifying accusations of sexual misconduct and abuse of children. Because I knew one priest at the time who had been falsely accused, I was asking Jesus what He does to support and comfort our brothers who had not done these things, yet found himself suddenly in the center of an investigation. It's become common practice for bishops to order temporary removal, and while that makes logical sense, my heart was grieving for the innocent victims as well as the innocent accused. While charges are sometimes dropped and names are legally "cleared," the public scandal of this grievous accusation has to remain associated with the crime in some people's minds forever.

Most of us don't have to be taught fear. And deep down, each of us has his/her own version of our worst nightmare: the most desperate, helpless situations that we can imagine. Wrestling with this topic, I sat in front of the tabernacle in church. I tried to imagine what it would be like to be accused of such a thing and actually be innocent. The tragedy that overwhelms the mind when an accusation becomes known can so easily lead people to presume guilt instead of innocence. That's exactly what Christ Jesus went through, for He **was** the innocent one but went through total humiliation and suffering to redeem us all. So I asked the Lord, "What would you say…to address this kind of situation??"

This lyric was the response…

Never forget, my brother, you're a priest of mine
From the crush of the vineyard, by my grace I make new wine…
As you come into my presence, other Christ, you're my delight
Rest before this mystery divine, that you're a Priest of Mine
From the day I ordained you, even long before your birth
My own heart conceived your priesthood
None can comprehend its worth
Come before me with your worries, trust my will, say "let it be"…
Share with me the joys and burdens of your mind
'Cause you're a Priest of Mine.

Don't despair, my brother, I'm the only perfect one
Hold the hand of my mother and keep your eyes upon her Son
Come to me—I know your pain…I will make your losses gain
Be a "fool for the Gospel" and you'll find
That you're a Priest of Mine

Let my presence fill your days, in your soul you'll sing my name
Take up crosses for my glory ,seek humility, not fame
Let my mother wrap her mantle like a vestment on your heart…
I'll make your struggle and your sacrifice a sign
That you're a Priest of Mine

The first time I ever sang this song was an amazing God-incidence (for those of us who believe that coincidences are usually just God's way of surprising us). After meeting Sr. Briege McKenna, OSC and Fr. Kevin Scallon, CM when they did a parish retreat during my ministry at St. Gregory the Great parish in Williamsville, they invited me to come to their retreat for priests called the Intercession for Priests. It's been held annually in Dublin's All Hallows College for over three decades, and the gist of the style of prayer is to fortify priests in fraternity, as true brothers in ministry. The importance of intercessory prayer as a way of uniting the ordained ministers during these wonderful gatherings has become an invaluable tool to support priests in our troubled times.

When I finished *Priest of Mine*, the Intercession seemed like the best place to sing it. Like countless other Catholics, Sr. Briege and Fr. Kevin were praying in reparation for the victims of sexual abuse by priests, as well as continuing their healing ministry for the daily bumps, bruises, and sometimes major heart-breaks and disappointments that priests face in their lives of service. The Intercession is an awesome week of retreat and prayer, and as a priest I thoroughly enjoy the camaraderie of the Irish clergy. The music is excellent, too, and that's always a plus.

Toward the end of the week of Intercession in August 2003, after having mentioned to Fr. Kevin and Sr. Briege that I had a new song that I really hoped to share, I realized on Friday morning that there was only one more Mass at which I might sing it. Entering the sacristy, I came across the retreat's music director Ephraim Feeley who was rather feverishly sorting out music for the upcoming liturgy. He seemed a bit out of sorts, and when I collected the courage to offer to sing a song, he was relieved. It happened that he had organized everything else in the week but that Mass, so my last-minute offer was welcomed.

After a period of silence following Holy Communion, I went to the keyboard, said a prayer, and took a very deep breath. This particular song's lyrics are actually difficult to sing without the emotion of the message overwhelming me. And it would be the first time I ever sang it in front of anyone but God. So here I found myself in a group of my peers in ministry, but I soon sensed something deep in me being prepared for this particular moment. I sang and played it, and then sat very still during several moments of silence. It was one of those interludes in prayer that you hesitate to break. In the quiet, what struck me was that it was as though Jesus sang those words, borrowing my voice, like he ministered some encouragement to the weary Irish clergy. And I try to remember to tell Him that He can do that any time...after all, He made the instrument!

Later that day, Sr. Briege pulled me aside to share that a young priest from a near-by diocese had arrived just in time for Mass that morning. He was not able to attend any other day of the week, because of life-altering news that he received the day before. An abuse accusation against him had been brought to the bishop, and he was immediately placed on leave for a period of investigation. He'd called All Hallows the night before, rather desperately desiring to meet and pray with Ireland's "healing nun" and her co-worker in the Lord's vineyard, Fr. Kevin. They suggested that he come for Mass, that they would meet with him privately afterwards.

When this priest heard *Priest of Mine*, he said that he felt it was written just for him and that the Lord had brought him there for that very reason. Within a few weeks of investigation, his accuser admitted that it was a false accusation, so he was exonerated and returned to his parish. I returned to Buffalo, in complete awe of the God who helped me find "my song" and even, by His generous grace, made it **another** priests' "song" for healing in troubled times.

Chapter Four

THINGS ARE NOT WHAT THEY SEEM TO BE

It's an adage of sorts that makes sense: what we see is not always the whole story. What we hear or feel may not ever be the total picture either, and the Lord God has control over it…if we let Him. I read somewhere that a fact-finder counted the number of times Jesus says 'Be not afraid" in the Gospels, and it comes to 365. Once for each day of our years. That makes sense to me. And it's a kind of spiritual vitamin for trusting Him.

Of course, often our discussion of the nutrients needed in our daily diet refers to deficiencies that call for a supplement. My life is that way, with the lived attempt to trust my maker and not let fear get the best of me. Some people run to the movies when a film comes out that promises to frighten you. I say…when I want that kind of fright, I just look at the coming month's calendar!

I remember a night about twelve years ago when I had one of those sudden moments of terror that I imagine people whose foot gets caught under a train track get when they hear a whistle and see a light coming at them. Can you tell that both of my grandfathers worked on the railroad??

There was a Healing Mass in South West Florida. Fr. McAlear had invited the music ministry from St. Luke's Mission to join him for a week of ministry in a place much sunnier and considerably warmer than Buffalo in winter. No-brainer, we say! The church was packed, and Fr. Mac had just finished a lovely homily on everybody's basic need for healing. The Mass progressed; the Prayers of the Faithful were read, and as he began the prayers over the gifts of bread and wine we call the Offertory, I was standing at his left.

Suddenly, a rather large man in a raincoat started to walk up the steps into the sanctuary. He was sweating profusely, and his eyes were rolling around. Something in my emergency-response system hit an alarm. What was this dude doing lurching toward us? I took a breath and prepared for anything. Then, he suddenly reached in the pocket of his raincoat and started fumbling for something. My heart stopped. Does he have a gun?? In an instantaneous panic, I looked at the stone altar and thought "drop down under there and you won't get shot!"

Then the man shouted out, interrupting the prayer of the Mass "My doctor says I'm going blind!!!" as he pulled out a pair of sunglasses and waved them, breaking into sobs. Relieved that he wasn't about to mow us down, I started breathing again and prayed for him as an usher quickly came up the steps and led him back to his seat. Is there an award for "Usher of the Century??"

Later, I shared with Fr. McAlear that I thought we were about to join the Lord! I confessed afterwards that I could have been more selfless and acted like a Secret Service Concelebrant, jumping in to shield him from the imaginary bullets. I laughed about the fact that I was blinder than the man losing his sight, and how quickly fear...which Jesus says is "useless" can cause a panic.

Several years later, I had a much more real and dramatic brush with fear. Fr. Joseph Bertha and I had visited Ireland,

and had to board a flight from Dublin at an hour when God himself is still hitting the snooze alarm. We checked our baggage, went through the shoe-less, belt-less X-Rays and arrived at the gate in plenty of time. Needing coffee like Jerry Lewis at the end of the Labor Day Telethon and gum for the ear-pressure symphony of flight, I headed into an airport gift shop.

As I rounded a rack of paperback books (mostly romance novels: Who the heck wants to be caught reading THAT if the plane goes down??) I passed a burly-looking Irishman in a rugby shirt. He looked as though he had just come from the stadium after an all-night Irish football tournament....and his team had lost...badly!

I heard a strange sound of a guttural, grunting stream of expletives and suddenly realized that he was talking to me. My pulse raced (guess I didn't need coffee after all...) as he snarled at me as if I had killed his mother, kidnapped his puppy and fired him from his job all at once. While I have a deep affection for the sound of the Irish brogue, I could only understand every two or three words. Guess I'd never heard a brogue speak such hatred and venom until that moment!

He was fuming about "what you priests do to children," a phrase that pierced me to the core. Ireland has been more than devastated by the tragic, horrific sins of priests who sexually abused children. And it suddenly occurred to me that my clergy attire at 5:30 AM was not something this man wanted to see....not just at the airport but ever! I was frozen in time, and he just kept spewing his rage.

Looking back, I don't think I had ever felt such danger of being physically beaten or even killed. All my mind could do was think "I don't know you...and you don't know me. What the heck IS this??" I thank God now that whatever county and town of Ireland he came from spoke a dialect of English that was incomprehensible or I might have been even more terrified. Somehow, I started to move away slowly and muttered "I don't know what you're saying…."

When I quickly walked into the crowded gift shop, I walked around a rack of Irish souvenirs and started to tremble, praying I would not be followed by this behemoth chap. My mind raced with "say your act of contrition," "HELP me, Jesus!" and at the same time… "Those poor people…look what the sins of priests have done!" Then, my sense of humor kicked in: "WHY didn't I start lifting weights in high school?" "I *don't* think I should try to sell him one of my CDs…" and "I should have stayed a File Clerk!!!"

Shake Well Before Opening

There's another kind of fear that is very natural, and it's very common. The fear of failure and humiliation. It keeps many people from ever trying what they secretly believe could be a very fulfilling experience. I'd call this type of circumstance a "God of surprises" moment.

When I was first ordained, my preparation for preaching was painstaking. I would prepare all week for a Sunday or Holy Day, and weeks for Christmas or Easter. I've always used a brief outline to try to keep my thoughts in some kind of flow; beginning, middle, and (when the congregation has prayed for it long enough…or the Spirit so moves me to it…) the end.

Once, I arrived to concelebrate an evening Mass where my friends in Voices of Mercy were singing. Honestly, my motivation was probably less than impressive. We used to go out to eat afterwards, and I was probably just a little lonely that day. Monsignor Ron Sciera was the pastor and celebrant, and he welcomed me. We made pleasant conversation, and just as the altar server rang the bell to begin, he turned to me and said:"The Lord wants *you* to preach tonight." Immediately, the bell rang, and off we went.

With no preparation, no notes, and very little if any confidence I walked into the situation thinking "Uh-oh....I've never done THIS before!!" The blessing in this was that I've probably never listened so intently to the readings during Mass. It was as though I were floating in an ocean of desperation, and a voice was offering instructions on how to assemble the life raft! There was presence of mind enough to keep saying "Come, Holy Spirit!" in between thoughts that were more like "Thank God I don't know these people here...." and "I could start coughing and go out the side door to my car!!"

As God's sense of humor would have it, the homily time came and the words came, too. It felt like spiritual tightrope-walking. Was there a net? Sure---and my fear was indeed useless and distracting. Was the homily short? I really don't remember. But I was glad to have been given the grace to forgive Fr. Ron for surprising me. Well...he said "the Lord wants..." so how can I not say "yes ?"

There But For the Grace of GOTH Go I...

When I was a parochial vicar (assistant to the pastor) at St. Gregory the Great parish in Williamsville, NY, the largest parish in the diocese, one of my duties was to work with the Religious Education Program as "moderator". Massive numbers of children and teens who attended public school would participate in classes either on a weeknight or Saturday morning. Occasionally, I would receive a call from Joan Rischmiller, the Director of Religious Ed, that there was a student who "needed to meet with a priest". One occasion that I'll never forget was a teenage girl who really stood out among her peers. In fact, she would draw the attention of many people in that suburban neighborhood and her school by her choice of fashion: they called it gothic or "Goth" for short.

I made an appointment with her to meet in my office one day after school. Her religion teacher reported little or no participation in class, and a number of times where she expressed no belief in God, and no interest in the Church. That kind of teen rebellion is nothing new. But in this generation the clothing, make-up, and demeanor were a sea of black. Huge black pants, dyed black hair, fingernail polish, sometimes more piercings than a colander.

In praying before the meeting, I asked the Lord to help me look beyond her appearance. The idea then came not to sit in my office but to take a walk around the parish grounds. It was sunny and warm. (In Buffalo, we have to grab those moments when they come.) She agreed to walk with me. I began with a prayer, with no expectation that she would say 'Amen' at the end. My guess was right!

Instead of addressing her attitude in class, etc. first, I decided to ask what she was studying in school, whether she belonged to any clubs. Her responses were monotone and minimal. I told her about myself, and how glad I was to have lived through the teenage years. Then, I was inspired to ask a direct question.

"Do you think God loves people who wear all black clothing?" There was a pause, then with a voice that sounded like a girl younger than her age she said, "No." I stopped walking, abruptly, which forced her to do the same. I looked into her eyes, through a pound of mascara mask and said with a smile. " You don't think God loves people who dress all in black??" I gestured to my clerical shirt, black pants and penny loafers. "I guess I'm in trouble, then!"

She laughed. And I knew that a small crack in her protective armor had appeared. Humor was the best tool for that moment, it equalized us and broke the tension. We walked another ten or fifteen minutes, and I simply expressed that to God, and to me, it doesn't matter how she looked.

And with a tone as kind as I could express, I told her that her style brings attention, and maybe that was what we all need from time to time. I get attention I sometimes don't want (in airports at the crack of dawn from people who consider me an enemy) when I wear black, but that what's most important is the goodness inside of us.

Chapter Five

HOLY DUCT TAPE

Friends are a gift from God. We might think that it's just happenstance, or good luck, but I'm convinced that special friends are hand-picked by the Lord who knows what they can teach us. One of those most extraordinary gifts for me was my friend Wendy Marks.

She was born and raised near Syracuse, New York, and later attended college at Fredonia State, South of Buffalo. We were born the same year, five months and a few hundred miles apart. From the day we met, there was something rather immediately deep and spiritual about our relationship. It was like the old twins "separated at birth" syndrome, the way we connected and related.

Her vocation story is a book of its own, but I'll summarize it into a call that included wife, mother of two sons, and lay missionary at an amazing inner city mission in Buffalo called St. Luke's Mission of Mercy. St. Luke's was a Catholic parish for about 85 years, and was a casualty of city blight, the rampant spread of drugs, and the crime that comes with that. Amy Betros and Norman Paolini, two lay people with a deep love for the poor and abandoned (not unlike Mother Teresa) were inspired to purchase the closed-down

Holy Duct Tape

❧ ❧ ❧ ❧ ❧ ❧

Lord of love and grace…my attitude is heading South!
I cannot hold my tongue, so…duct tape my mouth!
Help me stop before I speak,
Give me pause so I can think and pray
Close tight my lips to keep me from
what I know I'm not supposed to say!
If only my own self-control were
thicker than a French-made crepe
I'd remember to use faith, hope and love
as much as that adhesive tape
So many times I heard myself speak too quick
Then get stuck in a rut.
Now I'm asking you Lord, I give you permission to
duct tape me shut!

church, rectory and convent and open a ministry that put the works of mercy into flesh for Buffalo's East Side. It has flourished, against all odds, for twenty years! Wendy felt the call about a year into the Mission's existence, and she responded with total abandon.

My involvement in the ministry at St. Luke's Mission came about very suddenly, while I was standing in line at the wake of our auxiliary Bishop's mother. Amy and Norm got in line directly behind me, and as we talked, I found myself invited to visit the Mission, say Mass and be a guest on their radio show. Wow—God moves fast when He wants to! And that was just the start. The roller coaster was just approaching the first hill, and once it got going, a wild and holy ride began!

Wendy and I probably met the first time that I celebrated Mass at St. Luke's. She had a great joy about her, a charisma, a gift of hospitality, especially for priests. As I recall, she smiled as I left that day and said "We're going to be seeing a *lot* of each other, Father Bill!" There was something so true and even prophetic in those words that it struck me with a little fear. In Wendy's zeal for the Kingdom of God, she could affirm and lovingly challenge you in a way that you often felt the Lord speaking directly to you with her sparkling blue Irish eyes. The joy of the Lord often seemed to bubble up and splash over those she served.

As a celibate priest who had only minor brushes with romantic encounters in my young life (and, admittedly, the vast majority were in my active imagination…) I have always been quite comfortable in relationships with women in ministry as their brother. After all, having three sisters, having worked in an office full of women, and now working in parishes where women tend to be generously present (religious, married, and single) for church ministry, it's a role with which I am most familiar.

But this friendship with Wendy was different from any of those prior experiences. All I can say to try to describe it is that if in any way I was hoping to be like St. Francis of Assisi in my attempt at serving the poor, she was to me like his companion, St. Clare. It was a holy compatibility of the soul, spirit, and heart. And it didn't hurt that we were of the same generation and shared cultural references in songs, movies and the historical events of our childhood, teen and college years were fairly close. Spiritually, we were always on the same page. A short-hand developed quickly, and everyday adventures in serving God were shared daily over the phone and in person often.

Wendy was so goofy at times that I would wonder whether she wasn't actually my long-lost twin. When we were sitting next to each other at some gathering, she would reach over and un-tie my shoe if I had my legs crossed. We would laugh so hard when sharing stories of how God surprised us each day that one of us would cry out "Stop---I can't take it!" As you read this, you may be thinking: "How naïve---there must have been some undercurrent in that relationship that was not pure." Unequivocally I can say, while I may have at one time thought I could throw a dead sparrow in the air and make it fly, I am most certain that this was a unique and godly friendship. No tabloid story here....

We could also switch over from silly, funny talk to serious and profound conversation on a dime. While Wendy was at times gifted with what is called "holy boldness," she also knew that her tendency to use humor (like my own) as occasionally sarcastic and cutting, could be hurtful. At one point, she said "I just keep begging Jesus to put **holy duct tape** over my mouth to keep me from speaking!!" I loved that image so much that I later wrote the song quoted at the start of this chapter.

The gifts of the Holy Spirit can be so mysterious and mystical that it's hard to describe them to people unless you've met someone whose life manifests them in some way. Wendy had an acute sense of the holy, which included well-tuned alarms for the demonic. She was very sensitive in spiritual matters and could get a good read on a person when she met them. At youth ministry gatherings, she'd point to one of the young men and whisper: "He's supposed to be a priest." She could also point out the people quietly serving the Lord each day without fanfare and point out their virtue and sincerity: "He/she is HO-LY," she'd say. Two syllables, and two bobs of her head for emphasis, her prematurely grey hair waving in agreement.

Soon after I got involved at St. Luke's (while still serving as an assistant to the pastor in my early assignments) I was invited to concelebrate a healing Mass. I had never been to one but knew that my mother attended some, and to be honest, I was a little hesitant around the charismatic style of prayer. After all, Irish people best express themselves in humor, story, and song....or so I thought!

Fr. Richard McAlear, an Oblate of Mary Immaculate, was the celebrant. He has travelled the world for many years doing healing ministry. Before Mass, he turned to me in the sacristy while we were vesting and asked if I would be praying over people. I gulped and tried to bow out of it politely, when someone said "Wendy can pray with you, Fr. Bill!" I instantly felt a little bit better, but still wondered what I had gotten myself into. I don't have the gift of tongues, and never applied for a membership card in the charismatic club. But I would describe myself as "charismatic-friendly."

"Just watch what Fr. McAlear does," Wendy said. So I did. He began to pray with people and they started immediately "resting in the spirit" on the floor. I looked at Wendy with a "HOW are WE supposed to do THAT" look, and she just smiled. "Ask the Holy Spirit to work through you, " she whispered. "C'mon, where's your faith? Just trust the Lord." And so it began. As we prayed, I noticed that some people were nervous coming forward. Not as nervous as I was, I thought. But as time went by, the sense of the shepherd calming the sheep overcame my self-consciousness. And the Shepherd calmed me, too!!

Wendy had a lot of spiritual gifts, one of which is called discernment of spirits. As people came for prayer and healing, she would turn and say "pray against self-condemnation" or "fear of death" and I would ask the Lord for words to encourage them. We became quite a team, and over the next few years, I was not afraid to do healing ministry as long as she was at my side.

That changed suddenly on June 13th, 2000. A group of us were signed up for a pilgrimage to Rome and Assisi for the Jubilee year, with our friend Fr. McAlear as the trip's Spiritual Director. Wendy wanted to go, but was in no financial state to pay as a missionary, so I paid for her trip. We met that morning for Mass at Precious Blood Parish, then set a time to get together at the airport for lunch before our flights to New York and the international connecting flight to Rome.

Because Wendy's ticket was purchased at a late date, her flight from Buffalo to New York was on another plane. A few pilgrims from our trip were also on it. After sharing lunch, we all hugged and said goodbye. Wendy was very excited about this journey, and she said with a smile to our friend Fr. Dan Young "See you in paradise!!" She and her husband, Lenny, had just returned from a few days in San Francisco, a gift from a priest who heard the Lord tell him in prayer that he should offer them that gift. Although they were also scheduled around the same time to move into a new house, recently donated to the Mission by another priest whose mother had passed away, they went.

In the midst of packing up the house and preparing for two trips, she and I sat on her couch one afternoon and talked. She was perplexed about the sudden demands of a lot of stress preparing for two trips and a move. We prayed together, and the image that came to me was, as no surprise to her, kind of silly but also meaningful. As she shared her sense of being overwhelmed, what came to my mind was her name. There is no St. Wendy, and the only person I ever knew with that name was the fictional character in Peter Pan. So I felt that the Holy Spirit was telling me that she should be like that Wendy, who took the hand of Peter Pan when she learned to fly. She should take the hand of her Jesus, and ask him to guide the coming days. After the California trip, she brought me back a souvenir that I will always treasure. In the gift shop of the hotel where she and Lenny stayed, she found a Peter Pan coloring and activity book. On the plane ride home, she re-wrote the story, crossing out the text and making it her own. Wendy had learned to fly by believing.

On the plane to New York City just a few days later, Wendy turned to our dear friend Karen Manspeaker in the seat next to her and asked: "Do you see the angels?" Now, that's not a question you could ask to just anyone, but both Karen and Wendy being women of great faith, it was sort of normal conversation. Karen didn't see angels, but it didn't alarm her. She just figured that God was giving Wendy a little glimpse of something beautiful as a consolation. But as she went on, the description of what she was seeing got more detailed.

"They're beautiful! Like nothing I've ever seen before. The colors are hard to describe. Like nothing I've ever seen. And they're flying all around the plane!" Karen praised the Lord for this gift and probably thought "I guess this pilgrimage will be really something special!" Wendy let out a long sigh, and rested her head on Karen's shoulder. Several minutes later when the captain announced preparation for landing, Karen tapped Wendy's arm to have her return her seat to its upright position. There was no response. We now know that those angels were messengers for Wendy's scheduled departure. She had departed before the plane landed. Those who knew and loved her have no doubt that she was taken to paradise at age 39. Her pilgrimage had the ultimate destination. And the amazing, colorful angels were her flight attendants.

At JFK airport an hour or so later, our group waited at the gate for the pilgrims from the other flight to arrive, and as quite a bit of time passed, it suddenly seemed too long since our planes took off just minutes apart. Then the announcer called my name over the public address system and told me to report to airport security. I quickly did, and they told me that one of the passengers had taken ill and was at a local hospital. The local police were coming to escort me to the emergency room of Jamaica-Queens Hospital, where I found Karen outside a triage unit. From the look on her face, I knew it was bad. Then she told me: Wendy was dead. The shock was more than anything I had ever known. I struggled to comfort her and come to accept this horrible loss in an unspeakable cloud of grief.

We went into the room and saw her body. We prayed for a while, and even laughed in one of those "If I don't laugh now I may never laugh again" desperate moments. But as we tried to picture her with the Lord she yearned to serve with her servant's heart, a spirit of God's love began to wrap us. I blessed her body, kissed her on the forehead and said something in my soul that strangely echoed what I would later find she said to Fr. Dan "See you in paradise…" I believed that I would, but there was something profoundly sad in that goodbye.

When we departed Buffalo, Karen's then-husband had brought two yellow roses; one for Karen, the other for Wendy. As we left the hospital to find our way back to the airport, she carried both roses. The yellow rose is said to stand for friendship. Wendy's middle name was actually Rose…so Wendy Rose was holding her namesake as she slipped from this life.

We ended up continuing on the pilgrimage, for I was actually scheduled to provide music on the journey. As a priest, it's a challenge when we are grieving, because people look to us to comfort them. It's the most humbling thing ever. All of a sudden, to about seventy strangers on two buses, I was "Poor Fr. Bill." In my innermost thoughts, it was that dreadful "poor me" of broken-heartedness that no one ever wants to experience. Yet we went to see and visit the most beautiful churches and shrines, and everywhere there seemed to be angels. In statue form, of course, but they became vivid reminders of Wendy's death and God's ministry of consoling us in our sorrow.

The place where I experienced the most healing was our time in Assisi. As I've mentioned, I saw my spiritual bond with Wendy as a kind of echo of Assisi's amazing Francis and Clare. Here I was walking in their footsteps, praying in their churches, and even visiting the Portiuncula where St. Francis died. As I played the beloved "Prayer of St. Francis" during our Assisi Masses, I could hardly get through the final phrase: "and in dying that we're born to eternal life." Ironically, the cathedral where the relics (human remains) of St. Clare lay was closed for construction due to damage from an earthquake. I silently quipped to the Lord "You knew I couldn't take *that* one…thanks, Jesus. I've got my own earthquake damage to deal with!"

In reflection, the personal loss of a best friend at age thirty-nine was a transformative experience. This special friend with whom I sang (with St. Luke's music ministry Voices of Mercy) prayed, worked, laughed, and shared many meals had been taken from this world in a matter of seconds. The collection of family and friends I now have in the Kingdom only makes me look forward to it more, until my time comes, whenever that may be. Healing comes with time, though the heart never forgets. And I'm firmly convinced that it's not supposed to.

For the first anniversary of her death in 2001 I wrote a song called "Wendy's Angels":

Lord, won't you give me a glimpse of Wendy's Angels?
I want to see the colors she spoke of
On the day you took her home.
And with a prayerful sigh, I can see her hands lifted high
Carried on a wing and a prayer, by Wendy's Angels.

The Usher and the Anniversary

June 13, 2001 was the first anniversary of Wendy's death. We had planned a special Mass at St. Luke's Mission in the evening to remember her. I was still serving at St. Gregory the Great in Williamsville, and my daytime hours were booked up like a normal day at St. Gregory's: morning Mass, various meetings, etc. We had a visiting missionary priest for lunch. With all that, she was very much on my mind, and as we all know, anniversaries of a sudden death can sometimes bring us back to re-living in our mind the events of that day.

During lunch, a phone call came that one of our church ushers had been rushed to the emergency room. The parish is next door to Millard Fillmore Suburban Hospital. In fact, you can see the E.R. from the kitchen window! I offered to go, ran to my car and got my sacramental oils that are kept in the glove compartment, and headed straight for the hospital.

Joe, the usher, had been discovered at home unconscious by his wife. With no apparent signs of illness, he was found to be not breathing. As I heard the story, a very familiar wave of emotion came over me. As I headed down the hall to the room where doctors were attempting to revive him, I mumbled under my breath, in a prayer "Lord, what is it with June 13th and these sudden departures???"

There was a team of medical personnel working on this poor man. I entered the room with my oils, and soon discovered a series of tubes and machines as well as a sea of bodies surrounding him. I worked my way up toward his head and reached in between a few nurses and medical professionals to anoint Joe. Then I said in a low voice "Wendy Rose Marks, on this your anniversary of going home to God, please intercede with me for this man. If the Lord wills to take him, come to greet him on the way. If he's meant to stay, ask the Lord to help us, Wendy!"

In an instant, as soon as my prayer finished, one of the doctors said "We have a pulse!!" Aware that my holy friend in Heaven loved to pray with me at Healing Masses, I smiled. As I walked back out to the waiting room to see his wife and family, I whispered: "Thanks, Wendy. Guess this anniversary will be more memorable than I thought!"

Joe the usher became known as Lazarus! And while the church process of declaring the sanctity of a deceased person as saint can be complex, for me, there was a sign that day and many times since, that Wendy Marks was, and is…HO-LY !

Lonely Lazarus

❧❧❧❧❧❧❧

I used to be known as the brother of Martha and Mary
But illness overtook my life… dead and buried.
Jesus came…and He raised me up
But Friday afternoon it came,
A message from Calvary.
They nailed my friend to a cross,
Charged Him with blasphemy.
O, my Lord… Innocent blood out-poured!

I'm poor lonely Lazarus, I should be glad to be alive
But I can't help feeling left behind, abandoned,
Enclosed in a tomb of sadness with a stinging in my eyes
As I long to be with the one who gave me life.

Chapter Six

LONELY LAZARUS

The Bethany Bunch, Martha, Mary and Lazarus, were the "go-to" friends of Jesus in the Gospels. It seems that when he wanted to be with the ones who always opened their door to him for a respite, a meal, some personal time with friends, their home was the place He chose. From Sacred Tradition, we believe that these two sisters and their brother were very close to Christ, but I often wonder which relationship came first; friends or disciples? Or did they both develop simultaneously?

While the "beloved disciple" who sat closest to Our Lord at the Last Supper could also be argued as Christ's best friend, Mary and Martha and their brother (who spent a few days in a tomb before Jesus raised him) seem to me to be more like personal friends first, disciples second. I also wonder if, during the years before the Gospels were written down and there was oral tradition of story-telling, there weren't some theories of another sister. Remember that when Jesus approached the tomb of Lazarus and before He said "Roll away the stone," someone commented: "***Shirley***, there will be a stench!" Most biblical interpretations say "Surely..." and...

of course I'm pulling your leg. (My mother used to respond to a joke like that with: did you hurt yourself reaching that far for a laugh? But an occasional stretch is good for you when you're writing—or reading a book.)

One year during Lent, I had preached on the Gospel where the miraculous raising of Lazarus occurs. As I prayed with the Scriptures, it came to me that Lazarus, though the wrappings were un-tied and he returned fully to life, would ultimately have to die again. We sometimes focus on the wonder of his resuscitation or the fact that Jesus wept, expressing that common human emotion in grief for a loved one's passing. But Lazarus would eventually die for good, or—as we believe, until the resurrection on the last day.

Then I found myself pondering raised Lazarus' response to the news of Jesus' crucifixion on Good Friday as it reached Bethany. There are no Gospel accounts of the hyper sister, "Martha, Martha" being plunged into sorrow, stopped in her tracks from multi-tasking mania. We don't hear of Mary sitting in shock at the spot where she once sat at Jesus' feet in their living room, intently listening to her friend Jesus. But they had to have heard and been terribly affected until the glorious good news of Easter reached the Bethany Bunch. And the once-dead brother, knowing from personal experience that His Lord had the power to raise the dead, had to have been dumbfounded.

Lazarus would have to wonder how the one who raised him could die, how his friend who was obviously so powerful would become so weak as to die himself. On the cross, one of the criminals hanging in crucifixion next to Jesus taunts him to "save himself", but the overwhelming, prevailing thought that I imagined in the mind of Lazarus as I wrote this song was abandonment. And perhaps even survivor's guilt, and it would have to be the ultimate version of that kind of agony for the left-behind, for Jesus had brought him back from the grave. Of all who knew and followed Jesus, only Lazarus knew that experience first-hand. Yes--he was unofficially the first fan of a Rolling Stone!

The dark and cold pain and agony of grief and mourning are something each of us will know many times over a lifetime. But unlike Lazarus, the average person has not been in our own actual tombs and heard the call to rise and come out. Yet we can see through analogy the need to work through grief's stages and somehow rise up to continue living our lives after a death. In my imagination, Lazarus can become an icon for the continuous dying and rising pattern for personal and spiritual growth in Christian faith. The seed that falls to the ground and dies, goes on to bear much fruit. Then with changing seasons the self-sacrificing pattern propels us as we pass the gift of life to the next generation, for as long as we live on Earth.

Besides Joe the usher whom I saw revived in the Emergency room on Wendy's first anniversary of death, I've met only one other person who fits the description of a modern Lazarus story. Christian singer-songwriter Mitch McVicker was in the car accident that took the life of Rich Mullins, his dear friend, Sept 19, 1997. Rich was a major creative artist of song in contemporary Christian music. At the same time, he provided a unique prophetic voice that challenged the "star system" of record labels and Christian magazines making music ministers into celebrities. He often did concerts in torn jeans and bare feet, in contrast to some of the flashier artists of his time. Rich Mullins was the real deal, unique in ways that would take another whole book to reflect upon properly.

My cassette and CD collection in the mid-to-late 1980s included everything Rich Mullins ever recorded. The day I heard the news of his death, my heart was very heavy and something in me finally understood more clearly what another songwriter once expressed as "the day the music died." Some of the reports of his passing included a mention that another passenger (Mitch McVicker) was also in the vehicle, but remained in an intensive care unit in critical condition. I said a quick prayer for this friend of Rich, as well as the band that he had recorded with called the Ragamuffins and his family.

On the first anniversary of his death, I organized a night of Rich Mullins music at St. Gregory the Great Church. We showed some video footage from a tribute tape (DVD was not born yet)! that included some of his music videos as well as interviews with several of his associates and family members. I asked a parish volunteer to make a large sympathy card to be signed by all who attended, which I later mailed to the Kid Brothers of St. Frank, an organization Rich founded for outreach to the children of Native Americans on a reservation in Window Rock, New Mexico. We said a prayer at the end for his friends, family, band, and fans who experienced the loss of a brilliant and gifted man. And then as I recall, I quickly added a prayer for "the person who was also involved in the accident, and was severely injured". Knowing my memory, I can be pretty sure I wouldn't have remembered Mitch's name that night. Nor did I know that he'd be living in the state of mind my song described for Lazarus in the time between Jesus' dying and rising.

Soon after our Rich Mullins night, I read in *Contemporary Christian Music* magazine that just before his death, Rich had finished producing a CD for Mitch McVicker, one of the Kid Brothers whom, they reported, was the man riding in the Jeep with him that tragic day. I marked my calendar for the CD release day, and bought it as soon as the store opened. (One of my favorite things to do on Tuesdays, my "attempted day off" has always been to pick up new music, for providentially they also release new products on Tuesday).

At the time, I was also co-hosting a weekly radio show called "Praying Twice" with my buddies Gregg Prince (our diocesan radio ministry dude) and Norm Paolini, co-director of St. Luke's Mission but known for years before that ministry as a singer-songwriter at the start of the "Jesus Music" era and beyond. We started playing tunes from Mitch's CD as soon as it was released, and kept asking our listeners to pray for him in his rehabilitation. There were no other updates on his condition for quite some time, and no such thing as a blog for updates on his condition, so we just kept praying for him, and enjoying his music.

About a year later, Gregg and I had media backstage passes for the Kingdom Bound Christian music festival held each summer at the Darien Lake amusement park. We were with Wendy Marks and Heather Boctor from St. Luke's hanging around in a tent near the main stage waiting for musicians to interview for sound bites that we could play on the radio show.

At one point, Gregg tapped my shoulder and pointed to two long-haired, T-shirt and jeans-clad young men who were coming toward us. "That's Mitch McVicker," he said. For a moment, the heat and humidity of August had slowed my response, as I unconsciously thought "Who's that…and does he have ice water to share???" Gregg called to Mitch and musician Brad Laher, who approached and started chatting with us. (The other media folk didn't have Gregg with them to "name that artist"). After introductions, we recorded our conversation, much of which didn't make the radio show because the noise in the tent made it hard to decipher words and we were still close enough to a tent where another band was playing loudly. But the many bursts of laughter came through nice and clear!

I remember asking Mitch about the still-tender topic of the death of his friend and his own recovery process. He shared that he had been in a coma for some time, had broken ribs, and had to learn to walk, speak, and sing again. Because of head trauma and nerve damage from the accident, he also suffered from double vision almost two years later, but he was healing ever-so-slowly. In that twenty minutes or so, I grew more and more impressed with this guy, and his courage to go back to making music. Later, I would reflect that he was probably the closest person to Lazarus I would ever know, having lost a close friend and surviving the same accident, recovering and dealing with life after coma's tomb. In almost fifteen years since, I continue to enjoy watching the Lord work through him and welcoming his music and ministry to parishes where I am assigned.

At this juncture of my friendship with Mitch/Lazarus, I cannot help but wonder whether a better analogy isn't cocoon to butterfly, restoration and a new life. His story continues to inspire us all to remember what God can do to bring us through our darkest and most challenging times. While I initially wrote "Lonely Lazarus" for a Good Friday homily, its meaning to has taken on greater depth through having met Mitch personally and being moved to see how God's grace can restore us.

Chapter Seven

A PRIESTLY HEART

When you first set foot, or dip your little toe, into the process of priestly formation, it can be like landing on a new planet. One small step for man, one giant leap of faith that your God had this in mind for you. On the other hand, there seem to be people who sit by the pool and keep their feet dry, and occasionally tell those around them that one of these days they'll dive right in. But the towel isn't needed, for they stay put. Maybe it's like that Gospel story where the person wants to be helped into the pool at Bethesda, but when the water rises, it feels like everybody else rushes in first. I am hardly in a position to judge another's delayed vocational response time with my history of excuses and answering other calls. The God of perfect Love, thankfully, isn't terribly offended when we put him on hold. After all, from eternity He sees the whole story, including the end!

As I applied for the seminary and participated in adventures like the all-day psychological exam, a seminarian was assigned to my parish for his pre-deacon Summer. Merrick J. Bendar was one of the friendliest, most outgoing people I've ever met. He had a zeal for life that just bubbled up and poured into every room that he entered. An extrovert's extrovert! Across the board, the people of the parish loved him. The elderly were delighted at his youthful enthusiasm, the young felt akin to his boundless energy. And as a person anticipating entrance into the formation system that he was about to graduate from, I saw him as a light at the end of the tunnel. Even though I hadn't even paid my toll or driven into the tunnel yet.

Merrick the seminarian was gifted with an appreciation for life because, as it ends up, he nearly lost his life as a young man. When in college seminary, he collapsed one day on the basketball court at Wadhams Hall in Ogdensburg, NY. Tests revealed that he had a rare disease of the heart that would eventually call for a transplant. You wouldn't know that from looking at him six years later. My pastor, Fr. Berg, was a mentor to Merrick in those seminary years, and while my new friend didn't care to draw attention to his past illness, gradually other people filled me in on the miracle that he lived.

Whenever I voiced a doubt or hesitation about the years of education before me, Merrick would immediately insist: "You can do this! You'll be great! " And I was very much reassured. I had never known anyone so young who had gone through a heart transplant. He even named his heart-- Lucas. I'm not sure if hospitals ever divulge the name of a donor, but it has to be an instantaneous friendship when someone saves your life by organ donation. As I recall, less than two years later, Fr. Merrick offered his first Mass for Lucas, the person whose heart lived on in a newly-ordained priest. And the priestly heart of Jesus beat in him, too. The one whose heart was pierced for us, who can work great miracles, began a new work in this particular priest.

The jubilation and rejoicing on his ordination day were supreme. For his mother and numerous siblings (their names all began with the letter M…Martial, Mitchell, Michelle, Moira, Mark…) and Fr. Merrick's many friends, May 12, 1997 was like a dream come true. The vestment that was made for him showed two hearts joined with a cross rising from it. The tables at the dinner/dance reception in our parish center had bright red Mylar balloons. I doubt that any party before or since---or ever—could match the joy of that day.

Merrick was very generous to me, personally. Not only did he laugh at my jokes….almost all the time… he visited me in seminary and took me out for pizza. His positive reinforcement of my vocation was like a fresh breath of the Holy Spirit. When I voiced fatigue at having to attend night classes "at my age…" or groused about petty things in community living, he'd make me laugh at myself. And, looking back, he made me want to be like him. Although I was several years older biologically, he became both my younger and older brother. I even went to Buffalo Bison's baseball games with him. When he first offered me a ticket, I tried to argue that I'm a waste of a ticket for sporting events. But he wouldn't take no for an answer, and gave me spirited play-by-plays throughout the game. His love for baseball was contagious. I loved watching him watch baseball, and ever-so-subtly tried to hide my anxiety that a foul ball would most certainly hit the head of the person in the stands who was too busy flagging down the popcorn salesperson to meet a baseball the hard, hardball way!

At about the same that time he was being ordained, my Aunt Edna got an idea to throw a fund-raising party for me. At age twenty-eight, my broken-down first car would not be able to endure the half-hour ride to our local seminary. Aunt Edna explained that she had attended and helped run many a fund-raiser for people who wrecked their cars because they drank too much. This cause, she figured, was something people could get behind. While it was humbling to see signs in the storefronts of my neighborhood for a fundraising event with my name on it, I was heading into a five-year period where I'd only be able to work ten weeks each Summer. The rest of the academic year, we had to rely on the kindness of strangers and our own ability to stretch a dollar.

The party at the Ironworkers Hall in West Seneca was a success. And we only had to explain to a few people that I was NOT the beneficiary of these funds due to any diagnosis of a dread disease. It was the unfortunately rare case of a priestly vocation! The money raised carried me through the next several years, and my friend Fr. Merrick was instrumental in my need for a better vehicle. With the gifts that he had received at his ordination, he was planning to buy a new car. He took me to lunch one day and offered to let me buy out the lease on his car, which was only about three years old. And he said that he would pay the sales tax himself from his ordination money. I was deeply touched but didn't want him spending his money on me. This young man had a gift of a strong will, and once he decided to offer me that help, there was no talking him out of it. So I drove the 'Merrick-mobile' all through my seminary years.

One of my favorite memories of Fr. Merrick was the day I discovered that every Superman has his kryptonite. Here's a guy who survived a deadly heart ailment and transplant and returned to full strength. He was a fantastic preacher, had a wonderful pastoral sense with people, seemingly he was invincible. But one day before the 11:00 AM Mass, Charlie Ball, an elderly gentleman who served as daily Mass sacristan, came in to report that some of the ladies had seen a mouse in the sanctuary. Merrick turned pale, and reacted in a panic like I had never seen. "Get a broom, get something and get it out of here. I'm NOT starting Mass 'til you find it"!

Charlie remained pretty calm and soon produced a broom and a cardboard box. Merrick turned to me "Can you do this? I don't like mice!" The church bells rang out the 11:00 hour…fittingly, the 11th hour for the mouse. I took the broom, headed out and went rodent-hunting in the house of God. It didn't take long to locate the little creature, as he scurried around the bottom of the altar steps. I followed, swinging the broom and missing him. When the chase took us past the tabernacle, I stopped to genuflect, then proceeded. A few seconds later, with the swing of broom that Merrick would have cheered for at the Bisons' baseball field, the mouse was still. I swept him into the box, where he regained consciousness. Charlie dutifully took the captive outside and released him back into the wild.

This event was one that Merrick would bring up to me many times over the years. It wasn't that he wanted to recall his Mickey-Phobia, but he was so tickled that I paused to genuflect before Jesus in the Blessed Sacrament as I pursued the unwelcome intruder to the sanctuary. We started Mass a few minutes late that day, and I was the altar server. The memory of the slapstick scene just before the liturgy made it nearly impossible not to smile as we celebrated the sacred ritual.

Somewhere in my photo collection there's a shot of me with Fr. Merrick the day of his ordination, and a similar one from several years later at mine. The vehicle I drove eventually aged out, but right about the time that I would have regular income and be able to buy myself a newer set of wheels. The vehicle that Merrick lived in was another story. In the years after a transplant, recipients take large doses of anti-rejection medications which affect their immune system. While the transplanted organ extends their life, their life expectancy is usually shorter because of these and other factors.

I heard the news that Fr. Merrick was diagnosed with leukemia while I was in my first assignment at St. Mary of the Lake. He would have to go through a bone marrow transplant to survive. After many prayers and a search for a match-donor, his brother Martial was the closest match. A wonderful book, "Nine Ms and a Mother Like No Other-Our Journey from Messed to Blessed" (published by iUniverse, 2009) tells the story in moving and inspiring detail. The bone marrow transplant was a success, too. It seemed that he was like a proverbial cat with nine lives, which makes me wonder why he didn't pounce on that mouse at St. Teresa's...

While May 12th had been for many of us a day of incredible gratitude and rejoicing when Fr. Merrick was ordained, by God's mysterious plan, it also became the date of his death. After beating leukemia, his Lucas heart began to fail. Doctors placed him on the heart transplant list once again, and it would have been one for the record books, as the first person to receive two hearts by transplant. But it was not meant to be. The significance of his date of death was not lost on any of us. At one point, it looked like the young seminarian with heart failure who would not live to become a priest. But he did, and he lived life with a sense of bonus time that inspired all who knew and loved him. Even in his hospital rooms in various facilities, he was quick to give a pep talk to other transplant patients, other people with cancer, and pray with them.

It was seven years to the day, from ordination as a Catholic priest to passage into eternity. Seven is a Biblical number for completion, even perfection. Fr. Merrick J. Bednar (whom I often called MJB, probably because it sounded like MLB, Major League Baseball...) continues to be an inspiration to people who might be tempted to let life get them down. His life was graced in ways that lifted people up and made them want to live each day as a gift. In my memories of him, I am in awe that the Lord allowed him to become a priest, serve others, show them compassion in sickness because he had been there, and smile through it all. His was a heart that resembled His savior because it radiated life, love and hope. My friend Fr. Merrick had a truly priestly heart.

Your Priestly Heart

⁌⁌

Your priestly heart, O Lord
Whispered into mine this call
Live to sacrifice and serve
Loving not just one, but all
You give consolation to my frustration
Through cross and crown and kiss
Daily life prostration in celebration
Holy feast, blending struggle and bliss

Your priestly heart, my Christ
Loves me now when I'm poor and weak
Die to self and rise again
Grace and mercy still mold the meek
You give this vocation illumination
For healing wounded souls
Daily consecration and manifestation
Of your will, that the shattered be whole

Your priestly heart, I love
Here abiding in sacrament
Come and stay my soul, be still
In His presence so radiant
Holy palpitation, with veneration
Through my silence, my groaning and song
Replace consternation with a peace sensation
To your heart my adoration belongs…
Your priestly heart, O Lord
Your priestly heart, my Christ,
Your priestly heart, I love…your priestly heart!

Chapter Eight

SPECIAL DELIVERY

As a boy of about five or six, I have a distant memory of being at the Erie County Fair with my family. It's amazing how the mind's filing system sometimes keeps only a few details, and they stand out with bold color and focus....and, thankfully, no paper cuts! On that day, I have no recollection of going on rides, eating cotton candy, or visiting the farm animal exhibits. I cannot even recall who else from my family was with me, but there's one particular moment of my life that got etched or tattooed into my being for life.

Looking back, I see myself on a picnic bench in a very large crowd of people. Over my head, mounted on a telephone pole was a sound system speaker, and Karen Carpenter's voice was serenading us in an early 1970's summer day with one of the many hit songs that the Carpenters had released. At the table next to me was a girl about twelve years old, and she looked very different from anyone I knew. What drew my attention was that she was crying; really, wailing. Her parents were calm, and explaining why she couldn't have whatever it is she wanted. Deep within myself, I sensed that there was something very different about this child. Hers wasn't like the cry of other children.

The sound of her voice and the look on her face paralyzed me for a moment. All I could think of is, "Someone please do *something* for that poor kid! She's breaking my heart!!" Mysteriously, I now know that God was calling me away from the instinctive first-response fear of the unknown, for she was what people used to call in another era "retarded". She probably had what is commonly referred to as Down Syndrome. For a person her size and age, it struck me that her loud cries and wails were atypical for someone at her physical stage of development. By that point, most of us have learned to mute our frustrations rather than cause a scene and draw attention to ourselves. Upon reflection now, it's that kind of social pressure that seems to lead us to swallow our feelings and feed our neurotic tendencies! All I knew at that moment was that I wanted to break away from my parents and siblings and buy the girl whatever she felt she needed so badly.

As we walked away from that scene, I would find that in my future contact with God's "special" children that day at the Fair would come back to my mind. Decades later, I have come to be deeply convicted that our Creator makes no mistakes, but that He wraps some of His gifts altogether differently. In my childhood I yearned, like most kids to be "grown up," to have the liberties that little children are simply not yet mature enough to handle. For the first decade of life, it didn't often occur to me to plan on what to do when grown up. The closest to a life-plan was a childish fantasy that formed from the time I got my first nickel allowance and walked to Melrose Street's corner store to buy "penny candy': I would get a job and spend all my money on candy. Rational? No. Naïve….yes….with sugar on top… and the cavities/fillings to prove that I tried it!

One of the kindest priests I've ever known was Fr. John Aurelio. He spent many years as the chaplain of a local facility for God's "special kids." Fr. John became a champion for the marginalized mentally-challenged people and applied what he learned while studying for his Masters in Social Work before he was ordained. Again--like my own story, the experiences of young adult life can be a cumulative bank for future ministry. In a time when those labeled "special" were not yet mainstreamed as today, he gave himself to the task of serving them. When he preached at parishes, (and eventually became pastor of the parish next to my home church) he could effectively show us that we're all slow in some ways, all developmentally limited, and in need of the grace of the Lord who loves all His children perfectly.

Fr. John's regular Sunday parish Masses at St. Catherine of Siena in West Seneca drew many people for his creative preaching gifts. The Masses with a homily for children kind of epitomized the sometimes wildly imaginative times of the late 1960's and 1970's. Right around the time I was having my first encounter with a "retarded" person, he was building a reputation for being a master at artistic preaching. The women of the parish even volunteered to make special vestments for the kids' Masses. (I'll admit, it was not universally admired by the more traditional Catholic folk, like me.) It was said that he would wear vestments that featured Raggedy Ann and Andy, and my friend Joan Graham made him a chasuble out of blue jean material, complete with a pocket in front with a monogrammed J for Jesus. Groovy! And now, thankfully, passé, but nonetheless, apparently effective in drawing the attention of the young.

Almost twenty years later, when I ended up in seminary and was required to seek a personal Spiritual Director, I approached him at St. John the Evangelist parish. I discovered that he was also a gifted confessor, and would regularly walk the mile and a quarter to meet him on Saturday afternoons "in the box." I still remember one penance he gave me: if I had a few dollars, I should stop at the grocery store and buy my family ice cream and hot fudge and treat them to sundaes. I did, and it was a great lesson to me that our post-confession penances are not punishment but an offering of thanks and praise, a celebration of sorts like the banquet thrown by the father of the prodigal son. But since we had no fattened calf, we got fat on hot fudge sundaes!

At the time I approached this gifted priest to request his spiritual direction, I discovered that many others had already sought his counsel, and he couldn't really add any more. But that all changed when he was re-assigned from that parish to our seminary as House Spiritual Director. He would be teaching the course on Preaching, doing seminars on spirituality and offering spiritual direction to seminarians. As I recall, the day his rented U-Haul showed up, I also appeared at the dormitory where he was in the process of moving in. I probably volunteered to help carry boxes (and had an impressive resume for that, having helped Fr. Kilian move many times!) and, at the first opportunity alone with him, I asked him to be my director. This time, it was part of his duties, and he said yes.

The first time I met and spoke with him, I told him my vocation story. He surprised me by saying "You know, in my time, we would have called you a 'retarded vocation' because you responded to the call at a later age than I did." Then, to my relief, he went on to say that since I studied and worked in fields other than church work, my vocation would somehow add something different and unique to the mix. He also was a "retarded vocation," having lived and worked in New York City as a Social Worker before entering priestly formation. I was in good company... though I've since concluded that the delays in my path were all part of the plan, and that my response was right on time, not late.

Another thing I enjoyed about Fr. John was his appreciation of my sense of humor. I had to be careful not to get into my comedic vein when I went for direction, or I would simply enjoy making him laugh for the hour. His laugh was loud and raspy and full. He'd throw back his head and let all the emotion out. I now realize that ministry to God's special children taught him to express joy without ever holding back. But then again, he would often remind me that he was Italian and I was Irish. He attributed much to our cultural heritages, and was prone to follow a long laugh with the line: "Quinlivan---you are *terminally* Irish!!" I'd respond: "Terminal? Well, I'd say that's not a bad way to die!"

A Lion's Tale

A friend from my high school musical years was Katie Wright. She was the daughter of one of my teachers, Alfred Wright, who taught English and Shakespeare. I took every one of his electives, because he was a great teacher and had a dry wit. Several years after my ordination, I had the honor of celebrating Mr. Wright's funeral. And just a few years after that, I received a call that Katie's sister, Mary had died.

Mary Wright was one of God's special children with Down Syndrome. From the love her family received from her and the lessons she taught them, I was deeply inspired as we met to plan Mary's funeral Mass. They said that she had a unique ability to, as they believed, "see" beyond our sight. Much like a blind or deaf person whose other senses are more acute, Mary seemed to be able to see into the Kingdom of God from her home in South Buffalo.

I'm sure that, at first, it un-nerved her family. They told me that some time after one of their aunts had passed away, Mary suddenly stood very still, paused and then announced "Aunt Peg's here!" No one else could see her, of course, and

84

the innocence of these "kids" is so child-like throughout their life span, even a hardened cynic could be convinced that she did see her. I've always loved the theory that infants and small children can see heavenly beings, but our way of reasoning teaches them to mute that as mere imagination.

One day, they told me, she glanced out the picture window in front of the house, looking up toward the sky, and said, with absolute certainty in her tone: "God's here!" Now, a deceased aunt's communication with her loved ones is one thing, but this really got her family's attention! With their permission, I used that story in my homily at her funeral. When we lose someone, when we gather to celebrate their Mass of Christian burial, Mary Wright's words bring us simple yet profound comfort in child-like faith. "God's here!"

While I am not one who sees visions or hears voices (but then how could I, with the radio station in my head playing music most of the time)! I had one unusual and very real experience during Mary Wright's funeral. One of Mary's great loves was the classic film "The Wizard of Oz", so I had made reference to that beloved movie, alluding to the journey we take in life, seeking the "home" that is God's eternal embrace. (I myself have seen the flick probably a hundred times, and had to control myself not to go off on flying monkeys and witches, as God's grace kept me in control).

Toward the end of the funeral liturgy, during the Holy Communion, I noticed the organist's unusually powerful voice. It was somewhat operatic, in the lower register, and with full and dramatic flourishes of vibrato. In my mind, in a moment of distraction, I thought to myself: "Gosh---He sounds like the 'Cowardly lion'..." A second or two later, I heard in my heart a female voice whisper "It's the king-of-da-forest" A shiver ran through me. While I only knew of Mary through her sister Kate's stories, and may not have ever had more than a momentary conversation with her, I would not have been able to recognize her voice easily. As I said, besides the music playing in my mind's CD player, I don't usually hear any whispers.

I started an internal debate with myself, whether to share this story with her family. My fear of sounding crazy has to be a small taste of what people who do hear prophecies and see apparitions go through: what will people think? Shouldn't I just keep this to myself? Have I over-dosed on Hollywood musicals? Should I give up "The Wizard of Oz" next Lent??? Later that morning, after the prayers at the cemetery, I gathered some Bert Lahr "C-ourage" and asked Katie to call her siblings together. With a little hesitation, I recounted what had happened...the organist's singing voice, my connecting it to the Cowardly Lion...the female, whispered voice. Then I asked, point-blank: "Do you think that was Mary?" Their response was unanimous and immediate: "Of course it was!" Experiences like that make me so glad I responded to my "retarded vocation," and aware that I've been blessed with "special" moments of grace. And it was also verification of one of my greatest hopes, that beyond the grave, we still have a sense of humor!

Chapter Nine

STATUES AND LIMITATIONS

It's amazing how God knows exactly the moments we truly need to be humbled, and His creativity knows no bounds. Rather than hearing the voice of one's guardian angel whisper "Uh---no, buddy. That's *not* going to work." we get to face momentary challenges, as well as the week-long and years-long kind, as these experiences reveal to us in not-so-subtle ways our personality quirks and faults. And our need for a savior!

A certain hand-crafted prize at a fund-raising event for St. Paul's church in Kenmore, NY caught my eye the instant I saw it. I said a little prayer when I dropped my ticket in. My mother raised us with the wisdom passed on from her father and various other family members who "liked the horses" (Not in the equestrian sense or aesthetic lover of animals/creation, but in the trifecta/Kentucky Derby sense). That wisdom included the well-known "You can't win unless you buy a ticket" as well as Mom's lesson that she learned from personal experience: "Don't gamble if you're going to be a sore loser."

My raffle ticket was chosen and I was suddenly the proud owner of a set of soft, stuffed nativity figures made from cotton printed pattern. Each figure had an image of the persons and animals in a Christmas crèche with deep, rich colors and a tiny cardboard base on which they could stand. My intention was to bring them into the Kindergarten class during Advent because all of the manger scenes I'd seen were the plaster statue kind (nice, but easily breakable, and thus off limits to 5-year olds.) I liked the idea that I could let them pass these around to look at closely. Tactile theology works well with Catholics, and my thought was that I could teach about the Word made flesh better with figures that were not hard as stone, but more soft like our skin and that of the animals.

When the hoped-for visit to the Kindergarten, my intellectual equals, came, I forgot about the great prize that I had won. Then, as I began to decorate my rectory room for Christmas, I re-discovered them and thought that it would be fun to use these instead as pass-around props during the children's homily at Christmas Mass. I prepared my words carefully, congratulating myself for discovering this fresh approach to preaching on the mystery of Christ's Incarnation while using terms familiar to kids: "soft, squishy, mushy" and so on. But one of my mother's proverbs would soon come to mind: don't break your arm patting yourself on the back...

The Christmas Eve homily started off great, and there was even an audible "Awwww..." from some of the parents and grandparents crowded into the church as I held up one of the stuffed crib figures and began to pass them around to the kids. I did my best to teach that Jesus came, choosing to become fully human, so, despite His divinity, His newborn human body as a tiny child was, like ours, "soft and squishy." (Yes, after years of theological study I'd come to develop a style of Sesame Street sermons.) After about six minutes when the kids' attention spans were apparently waning, I said "Okay, boys and girls, you can give back the nativity figures now..." In an instant, the crafted characters and cattle were catapulting toward me from all directions at once. The camel sailed over my head, the shepherd struck me near the heart, the Holy Family took flight long before they left for Egypt, and as I recall, the stuffed donkey (in fitting irony…) whacked me right in the face. The whole congregation burst into laughter, as I tried to recover my pride and composure in response to getting what I asked for, literally. And what I deserved, perhaps!

That evening at our family gathering and gift exchange, I sought my mother's sympathies at my public embarrassment. With a hearty laugh, she replied: "Serves you right, you dumbbell. You gave those kids ammunition, then asked them to give them back!" I don't think I've ever used those squishy nativity figures for the same purpose again, but every time I'm tempted to donate them or give them away, I don't. They are a soft reminder of a hard reality: we are called to come to the Lord like little children. And kids like to play catch!

Priests spend quite a bit of time with the elderly, and those who've taken care of aging parents know that at life's most advanced stages, they often become like children again. At Blessed Sacrament, our parish is responsible for the pastoral care of one of the local nursing homes. There are regularly scheduled Masses, distribution of ashes as Lent begins, and occasional anointings/prayers for the sick and dying. The room where they set up for Mass seems to have been designed by folks who represent the "Lollipop Guild" and follow yellow brick roads with friends who drop in. Volunteers must cram a number of wheelchair-bound persons into the tiniest quarters, and their creative parking skills are amazing.

Chandeliers are not the friends of people like myself at six feet and two inches tall. One day while preaching at the nursing home, I stepped around in front of the altar to make a point, and, practically, to be heard better by those with diminished audio capacity. When I stepped back, I smashed my head so hard on the hanging ceiling lamp that I saw a white-out like Buffalo January before my eyes. As the haze cleared, I could hear the most unusual, loud, guttural laughter. The woman having a grand laugh at my expense was someone who resided in a somewhat cloudy state of dementia part time. She apparently found my injury the most hilarious thing she had ever seen. In that moment, I quietly cursed the generation of comedians of physical pratfalls and slapstick comedy who give us permission to laugh at others' ouches as my head throbbed.

She had a voice like an animated Disney villain in slow-motion, cackling in almost slow motion: "Haaaaaaaa... haaaaaaaa... haaaaaaaa. He hit his head! Haaaaaaaa, haaaaa..." The extent of her delight bordered on demonic, as I wondered whether calling in an exorcist might be prudent, but soon realized that my ego was hurt more than my head. After Mass, I was able to see the humor in the situation. But I laughed nowhere near as heartily as Cruella De Villainess in the front row.

Mom lived in a skilled nursing facility for about seven years before her death at age 85 in 2008. When I went to visit many Sunday afternoons and on my days off, she loved to send me on missions to other residents. "Hi, honey. Did you bring your oils with you? Dolores in Room 16 is dying," or "Stanley's having his pacemaker adjusted tomorrow. Would you mind stopping in to bless him?" Of course, I didn't mind, but sometimes it's best to leave those duties to the facility chaplains. But I knew that she would have gone with me if she could walk, so my extra pastoral visits became a proximate expression of her kindness.

One visit in particular reminded me that it's sometimes best to page the chaplain. Visiting Mom on a Tuesday afternoon, we were casually chatting about the events of the day when we suddenly heard a new and un-familiar voice. It was a woman's voice, with a distinct Irish brogue. She was shouting repeatedly with panic and alarm: "Help me! Help me! Somebody help me!" As this kind of cry can be fairly common in elder care facilities, we waited a moment to see which of the attentive staff members would respond. But after a few minutes, it was impossible to continue our conversation, and also felt like torture to listen to her cries. Finally, Mom said, "Just go out and see what she needs 'til the aide comes!"

I found a feeble-looking lady in a wheelchair in the lounge area that was only about ten feet from Mom's door. At first, I was astounded that someone so small could produce sound so piercingly loud. The producers who hold auditions for the musical "*Annie*" have to have similar experiences with children who inherit the Ethel Merman "I don't–need-a-mic-with-these-lungs" gene. As I tried to calm her, I looked at her identification bracelet, and saw that her name **was** Annie (no kidding...) and asked her what was wrong. I was standing in front of her, and she finally started to gradually decrease her volume, thanks be to God. (My ability to hear was still needed for confessions, and besides, my auto club membership doesn't cover flat eardrums.)

"Help me..." she said, in a more conversational tone. Then her tone changed to an angrier one: "Where's the nurse??" Trying to calm her, I responded: "Someone's coming, I'm sure. They're probably helping another resident who needed something." She paused a moment, quiet for the first time since she drew our attention. So I thought maybe if I engaged her in conversation and stayed with her, she wouldn't be so upset. There was no apparent danger—she just had Henny Penny Syndrome where the sky was falling, and probably in that state of mind, with all due respect, it's as real as the anxious thoughts tell you.

"So, Annie, you're from Ireland, are you?" I said with a smile. "What county are your people from??" Her expression immediately soured, as if I had just told her that the menu of the day was prune casserole with vinegar gravy. She torqued up the volume again and barked at me: "Why don't you go visit the person you came to see!" So I did! Within seconds of being put in my place by a 100-year-old-lady, I returned to Mom's room and the litany of "Help me, Help me" resumed. A wonderful nurse named Jean came hurrying down the hall to Annie's rescue, and after only a moment, all was quiet again in the skilled nursing unit. You learn to enjoy such moments of calm, and more importantly to be thankful for the beyond-price skills of such caring professionals.

Annie lived several more years, rarely losing her gift of vocal projection. And my mother developed heroic patience from the day that she gained this unique next-door neighbor. I learned to find the nurses and aides myself if the human alarm system's noises drowned out our conversation. But I also must admit that we were fascinated at times by Annie's protestations of a more religious nature. Sometimes she'd decide that rather than call for the staff's attention she'd yell: "C'mon, Jesus. C'mon, c'mon, c'mon!!" (as if, after 102 years she was impatient waiting for her departure into eternity.) So, under my breath, I'd respond" "Lord, *hear her prayer*!!"

It's sometimes hard to stifle laughter which comes about in situations where you try with all your might not to let it out. When my father found something that tickled his funny bone in Church during Sunday Mass, suddenly we could all feel the pew shaking.

In California, they're trained how to respond to an earthquake tremor. We knew that the odds were against that, and marveled at our father's ability to chuckle without a sound. There'd be nothing audible at all, but we knew when Dad got the giggles. (I figured that, when he was a kid, there were silent movies....maybe audiences weren't allowed to laugh out loud) As we all know, the harder you try not to laugh in an inappropriate moment, the more impossible it seems to suppress it. And sometimes, the overwhelming need to scream with laughter gets frozen inside of us for a time, with whatever level of self-control holding back the dam.

When I was a seminarian, the parish where I served had a terrific music ministry for the contemporary style Mass. I used to sometimes join them, maybe to teach a song I knew that they wanted to learn. Or sometimes they were helping me increase my musical repertoire. One memorable night, we went to the home of one of the church's singers (who could also shake a tambourine with such spirit that would shame Tracy Partridge—from TV's fictitious "Partridge Family" -- into instant retirement). I was playing piano, and after about an hour of practice, without thinking, mentioned aloud to no one in particular than I often get a kink in my neck from the way I sit over the keys.

A woman in the group spoke up and said "My husband has that problem, too. Want me to do what I do to help him?" I was half-turned from the piano keys as she spoke, and before I could answer, she reached up the arm of her sweater and, with my peripheral vision I saw her pull off an artificial arm/prosthesis. Now, I had known her only a short time and did **not** know that she was an amputee. My instinct was to quickly turn back toward to the piano, and the next thing I knew, the back of my neck was being massaged…with the portion of her natural arm that remained.

I waited about 15 seconds and blurted out: "Oh…Gee— that feels *much* better. Thanks so much!!" All I could think was: "Quinlivan, if you've ever not let a nervous laugh coming out of you, now is the moment!" I just wanted this to be over, and was eternally grateful that I was facing toward a wall, for the look on my face would have certainly insulted my volunteer neck massage therapist. You simply cannot make these stories up…they just happen and you never see things like this coming. But I've gotten years of mileage out of telling this one, and tag it with a Joan Rivers-like one-liner of a title: "So…I call that story-----Stump the Band!"

Who Put the "Ha" in Abraham?

Surely you've heard, read, and experienced the wisdom that tells us that listening carefully is always important. Can you hear me, now? I'm typing as loudly as I can. Computer keyboards have such a polite sound, like my West Highland Terrier, Benny's paw taps on the kitchen linoleum signaling that a trim is due! Old-school typewriters were so much more expressive. If you pushed down on the key hard enough, you could actually punch a hole in the paper. Not that a peaceful, passive Irishman like me would know......

The calm, subtle approach works best with elderly and home-bound people during a pastoral visit; and for many, when the priest comes, it's a comforting sight. But sometimes when I enter a hospital room, I'm greeted with a look of terror, and I wonder: Did someone warn them in advance about my puns? Are they expecting me to sell them my latest CD? (Guess it's just too obvious to have them sticking out of my coat pocket....) I have to remember that for some of the faithful from my parents' generation, when they "called the priest" it meant you might be about to exit this earth. It's like the bus to eternity has pulled up at your door and the engine is idling. A few have actually responded to my initial entry and greeting with: "Am I THAT sick??? Nobody told me!!" So it's a relief to bring good news that I don't usually know what you're suffering from, or what the surgeon has removed or implanted. If I did, the Etch-A-Sketch could have been shaken in the elevator on the way up, and all information deleted. What I do ask people to remember is that I have no need to see their stitches.

Others, who perhaps in their church-going years never went out the center-front door where Father often stands at the end of Mass, seem anxious as if I plan to quiz them on Latin conjugations. (Not that I ever studied Latin... I always say the only Latin I know is "Gloria Estefan") Some have actually responded to my "Hello, Gladys" (or Irving....okay, maybe not Irving. The rabbi can visit him...) with "I couldn't get my envelopes in, Father, I've been in the hospital!" It tickles me to think that they picture me pouring over the parish donation records before responding to a sick call. ("Oh, Lord...another cheapskate. I'll pray for a healing of their generosity ...") In truth, I am blissfully ignorant of those figures. At parish Finance Council meetings, the numbers are totaled before I see them, and I do not count the collection.

One of my favorite visits was to the home of a lovely older lady whose ability to hear was extremely diminished. She started her part of the conversation loudly shouting: "Sorry I haven't been able to get to Church, Father! Two knee replacements. And the nurse hasn't come yet today...and I can't find my hearing aids."   "No problem," I said, "you know, we miss you at Church but hope you're able to come back soon. And I'm so grateful to Anita for bringing you Communion."   She smiled a moment, trying to process that thought, or, more likely, attempting to read my lips.

"Oh, she's great!" the lady said. "Yesterday she gave me an enema!" My first thought was: Wow, those Eucharistic Ministers at our parish really go beyond the call of duty!! Then I realized that she thought I was talking about her nurse.   I fought with all my might to keep the conversation that I continued internally from being voiced: "Well, doesn't the Bible say 'Love your enemas?' Or was that enemies?" Thankfully, I succeeded in being silent! Besides, quips to the nearly deaf are seldom understood, or appreciated. The cliché says that silence is golden, so I dropped another coin in self-control's tip jar.

Parish secretaries deal with the most bizarre situations with ease. The phone calls that come must be fielded like rapid-fire slap-shots on goalies in the Stanley Cup finals. In former times, I'm told, parishioners were often more afraid of dealing with the secretary than the pastor. She was often like his Enforcer: "You want to talk to Father? You gotta get through me!"

I delight at hearing church secretaries tell of their skill-building and virtue of self-control. On December 24th, legend has it that endless calls inquiring: "What time is Midnight Mass?" (After Pope Benedict XVI changed it to 10 PM at the Vatican, many pastors followed suit. But in times gone by, the answer was *really* "midnight.")

When I was newly-ordained, a call came to the rectory office from someone who had heard that I used to be a comedy writer. They wanted me to give a talk on God's sense of humor.

Caller: Do you have a funny priest at your church?

Secretary: (Deadpan) Strange funny or ha-ha funny? We have one of each!

While preparing that talk on holy humor, it struck me that God reveals this awesome aspect of His personality in subtle ways. In the familiar story of the patriarch Abraham, the Holy Bible teaches us that his name was originally Abram. But the Lord changed it to Abraham, and one day it occurred to me that the two letters inserted were actually "HA!" (Okay, you Biblical literalists… it could also be "AH!" But I'll leave that interpretation to doctors examining tonsils.)

Abraham's wife had a name change, too: Sarah was formerly Sarai. I'm convinced that she could have been the first Jewish stand-up comedian if the scripture writers had the nerve to record her one-liners when God's promise of a son came through when she was in her nineties. If I were still writing for Joan instead of Jesus, I could pile up a number of ten-dollar paychecks on that!

My friend, the late Fr. Ted Berg was pastor of my home parish, St. Teresa's at the time of my ordination. He teased me mercilessly on my number of "older lady friends" who reacted to my arrival like fans at a teen idol autograph party.

When my first collection of songs, "Paintbrush in the Green" was released, I could hear him saying: "Will it be available on 78 RPM for your core audience??" A very good question. The 8-track generation wouldn't be interested, I know. But I stepped out in faith like Abram before the "HA" and somehow sold a few albums, I mean compact discs.

Some people re-define age through decades of practice in graceful aging. Mrs. Lillian Nichter was one of the most amazing people I've ever known. When I arrived at Blessed Sacrament Church, she was a very involved 95-year old parishioner. In 2012, she died at 103 years young after a very full and faithful life. Our age difference never stood between us, and I knew she was hip when my first CD came out because she pulled me aside and told me "I listen to it **every day**!" That touched me deeply, for what she found in the songs was hopefully opportunities to pray. She also purchased several copies to share with friends and family, so I appreciated her also taking opportunities to pay as well as pray, since the parish benefited from the sales.

My interaction with elderly ladies continues to give "fodder for Father" to recount unusual interactions. Last year, I visited a parishioner in a dementia unit of a local senior care facility. I always know where to find her---in the activity room, where a sweet young lady who is Activities Director uses music to reach her patients' hearts. I usually sit next to Freda, who was our beloved votive candle manager for years. She faithfully removed the empty glass bottles and arranged the fresh new ones in appropriately seasonal color-coded displays.

One recent visit with Freda brought yet another unique experience from the "You just can't make this stuff up" file. When I arrived at the Activity Room and approached to greet her, the lady in the chair next to her reached up and yanked on my sleeve. "Hey!" she said.. "Can you do THIS?" and she proceeded to push out her dentures and click them like a loud round of ammunition being fired, like those plastic clattering teeth that they sell in novelty stores. I was a bit stunned. Just when you think you've heard every theological question…a new one comes up! After a moment's pause, I simply said "No, honey, I can't…. but *you* sure do it well!" When I left a while later, she gave me another Poly-grip-free salute. The Lord works in mysterious ways.

Listen to this one…oh, yeah. Read on… When I was a seminarian, I always found great and profound joy at attending ordinations. The process of priestly formation from my formal application to my own ordination day was about six years. So as I moved through the years of study and ministry training, I was blessed to befriend a number of those who were in the classes ahead of me. When it came time to assign servers for ordination day, it was often the under-classmen. Serving on the altar very often meant a wonderful point of view for the bishop laying hands on the man being ordained, the consecration and anointing of his hands, and various other parts of the sacramental celebration.

In seminary years, your only paid work was a ten-week Summer assignment in a parish. The rest of the year, money had to be managed carefully. So when an ordination was out of town it usually meant several of us sharing a hotel room. Once, we travelled to New Jersey for a priesthood ordination. Our frugality by necessity meant setting a near-record for the number of persons crammed into one costly hotel room.

The most vivid memory from that trip was being suddenly awakened by the sound of a blood-curdling scream in our room in the pitch-black dead of night. One of us was apparently having a terrifying nightmare. (And I am under a long-term self-imposed friendship vow not to publicly divulge his identity…so, don't worry if you're reading this….but you and the other ten of us know who you are!!) In the heart-stopping aftermath, there were a variety of different responses. One guy fell right out of bed onto the floor.

(Those fire safety and emergency preparedness assemblies in school certainly taught him well to "stop-drop-and-roll.") Everybody else sat straight up in their beds, roll-away cots and couches.

After the scream ended and the loud thud of Tom hitting the floor passed, there was about a five-second silence. Though we couldn't see a thing, we slowly realized that the friend with the frightful dream was the guy I loved to tease for his penny-pinching, coupon-loving ways. My one-liner training kicked in: "Did you dream that we put the hotel bill on *your* credit card?"

Meat Raffles And Bowling Balls

My mother often used to tell me "you have to learn to dance!" Not that I had no rhythm. I actually took a Ballroom Dance elective as a gym class at Buffalo State and got an A. She was talking about the kind of dancing around and side-stepping situations where well-meaning people invite you to social gatherings that might turn into a real, live scream-inducing nightmare if you don't acquire the ability to say "Thanks, but no thanks." My friend Colleen Higgins and her family have a great line that I now quote. When invited to an event that would be considered a painful waste of time, you say; "Oh, I can't make that. It's the night I polish my bowling ball!" The way I learned how that applies was in her responses to my invitations to our parish's meat raffles.

Admittedly, raffling off meat is not as enticing to most people as a cash give-away, or a new car, or tickets for a cruise. It took me several years of driving past other church halls where meat raffles were advertised to consider finally hosting one at my parish. But from the first one, many of us were hooked. It's hard to imagine the excitement of a few hundred people cheering as a wheel spins, waiting to hear if they've won a frozen pot roast or ten pounds of frozen hamburgers. I find myself laughing through most of the night. Seriously, as a non-drinking Irishman, though, I quickly realized that the beer has an effect on the sudden appeal of the carnivore carnivals.

After several seasons of Meat Raffle invitations, I finally promised Colleen that if she came to one of our events and didn't like it, I would stop inviting her. I would even pay to have her bowling ball professionally polished for her. So— she came to one, and when I greeted her with joy and a sense of accomplishment (getting another Irish person to change her mind…no small task)! she pulled out her bowling bag. The ball wasn't inside…thankfully. So she had something to bring home her five pounds of frozen spare ribs. Not since Eve has a spare rib brought about such an enthusiastic response.

Chapter Ten

FOOTPRINTS OF GOD

My taste in music falls into a category that radio programmers used to call "middle of the road." In the 1970's and 80's they called it "soft rock," which sounds like something you could drop on your foot and not cause any injury. The easy-listening or contemporary sounds come nowhere near the head-banger, heavy metal rock and roll. I have never grown my hair into a mullet...the very thought of it probably has people who know me grinning as they read this. Delete that thought! It's not gonna happen!!

Pop music has a quality that, they say, has a "hook", a melodic pattern that catches your ear and gets into your head. They say that's what hit records are made of. But being able to craft more than one hit record is more difficult than it may seem on the surface. When recording my CDs, I do listen with the inner voice of the music lover who wore out many a needle on a stereo by re-playing certain 45s and records. And a collection of songs needs some changes in tempo to keep the listener's attention from start to finish. So I aim for a mix of tunes with a variety of tempos.

Footprints of God

⧉⧉⧉⧉⧉⧉

Do you wanna tip-toe, do you wanna run?
Slippin' on a sheet of ice or strollin' in the sun?
Trying to make your own way, or be a faithful one,
Try walkin' in the Footprints of God.

Heaven help me somehow, move my feet an inch
So I'm soaring like an eagle ,instead of flappin' like a finch
Some days just like new shoes, they give your feet a pinch
While walkin' in the Footprints of God!

Just as there are labels for musical styles, it's also common to use labels/titles/categories for styles of faith and belief within church circles. I remember finding this most repugnant when I first encountered it. "She's conservative... he's a liberal.." gets quickly tiresome, to me. Probably because these titles have such a political overtone, I avoid them. But that doesn't mean I can keep others from slapping the label on me.

In Catholic life, in my preaching, I prefer "faithful" as a term I encourage my parishioners to aim for in our daily walk with Christ. That seems to be the kind of description that's worth working toward. Is it not true that both ends of the political spectrum can be quite extreme and ugly, and come across as judgmental, condemning and un-loving? I love the music of Diana Ross and the Supremes, but I don't care to be associated with Dyna Mite and the Extremes.

My sense is that Jesus wants the members of His Church to aim for the middle of the road. Yes, there are issues for which we have clear moral guidelines and teachings. Faithfulness seeks to accept them, internalize them, and live according to the dictates of a well-formed (and especially *informed*) conscience. We are certainly called to be witnesses to Jesus, and the way we project our faith's presence says a lot about how well we know Him. There are things I will write letters for and against in the political and social realm, and applaud those who have a passion to take up a cause. But it seems to me that self-righteousness can so subtly overshadow the virtue in that kind of work if we aren't really careful and prayerful.

About half-way through my seminary years, a new classmate joined us. He was in formation for the Barnabite order, the Clerics Regular of St. Paul who minister at Our Lady of Fatima Shrine in Lewiston, New York, just north of Niagara Falls. Richard's response to his priestly call came at an even more mature age than mine. He was at the time a recently- retired high school English teacher with a sharp wit. Only a few weeks after his arrival at our seminary, he had given several of the seminarians literary giant pseudonyms for their apparent resemblance to classic authors. I was dubbed "a young James Joyce." Not a bad choice when you consider that he named another guy "an emaciated Rudyard Kipling."

Almost two decades after our priestly ordinations, Fr. Richard and I are still good friends. I credit him in our mature student years for helping me put into perspective the tossing of labels like "liberal" and "conservative" for what it was, and is. People don't always trust those who hold opinions (theological or otherwise) drastically different from their own. It's sometimes just old-fashioned human insecurity, right, left or center! And high school English teachers seem to be able to read people as well as the books they assign. Fr. Richard also has a delightful tendency to give spontaneous oral presentations of a "book report" on you as he gets to know you better. At the same time, he honors the fact that our present state is sometimes just a work in progress or draft of the final publication!

One day, during one of our extended conversations in my dorm room, he got my attention with a comment that has stayed with me to this day. After I expressed an opinion on an issue we were discussing I can hardly recall now, he stated, in his unique professorial pontification mixed with affection: "Bill, you're an enigma!" At first, I quickly thought "Oh, no...can't remember what that means. Is it good to be an enigma or should I confess that the next time I go to confession?? Enigma... isn't that what you take for constipation?? Oh, no that's enema..."

He continued: "Just when I think I've figured Bill Quinlivan out and come to the conclusion that you're a conservative... you say something that might just mean you're more liberal than anybody else here. You're difficult to label, you keep surprising me!" My response: "Thank you—

that's a great compliment." So I realized that day exactly why I prefer not to wear a label; that it limits my free will and conscience. The middle of the road seems to be a healthy place to walk. Isn't the middle of a paved highway the highest spot, so that water and mud can run off to the sides into the gutters? From the center, one can see and reach out to both directions, even the extremes, and invite them together. Remember, Jesus is traditionally depicted in the passion scriptures, on the cross hanging in the middle of two thieves, literally between Heaven and Earth….our Divine Middle Man!

The two thieves crucified beside Him were both guilty, as we humans can be. Both had the equal, though brief moment of opportunity to recognize the Lord. One of them cried out "Jesus, remember me when you come into your Kingdom." And Christ assured him that "This day you will be with me in paradise." The other…only God knows where he ended up. The Scripture doesn't report anything other than his spoken words. In his heart, I like to remember that he still could have cried for Mercy and been embraced by the one who died in the middle of them, for them and us. I prefer to hope that the ones most easily labeled as condemned and guilty can still be saved by God's final choice. If that makes me an enigma, I'm happy to fail on the side of Mercy! And if I'm wrong, that same Mercy will be good to me.

Spiking a Musical Temperature

At times, my musical tastes leave the middle of the road, but usually my mental MapQuest soon gets me back where I started. In June of 1978, my senior prom was just at the point when disco music had peaked and the record albums were beginning to be burned in public. So, to me, suddenly it seemed more appealing! Besides being an enigma, I am also someone who doesn't follow trends because being "cutting edge" has hardly been my life's goal. But right after a trend, the things that once sold like hotcakes are marked down like day-old bread. You can still slice day-old bread, even if you borrow yesterday's cutting edge.

Fast forward thirty years from my discovery of the disco sound to a pilgrimage that brought me to the tiny country town of Ars, France. In 2009, Pope Benedict XVI had called for a "Year of the Priest," and Fr. Joseph Bertha and I decided to attend an International Priests Retreat in Ars. In addition to developing an immediate addiction to chocolate mousse in its' mother land, the trek to France had other delights in store. There were shrines and churches I had never seen, so we rented a car and headed out into the countryside when the retreat ended.

On Sunday, we were relying on the GPS to help us find the town of Nevers, where the great St. Bernadette of Lourdes was interred in a glass sarcophagus, or see-through coffin. (Most people recall the way Snow White was laid out under glass after she ate the poison apple. But Catholic saints have been reposed that way for centuries.) It was about a two and an half hour drive, and we stopped at several Catholic churches that morning until we found one where we could concelebrate Mass. If my ability to read the GPS directions were as attuned as my taste buds for mousse, we would have arrived in a more timely fashion. The font on Fr. Joseph's cell phone which displayed the directions (thanks to satellite technology) said to head North for 3.5 miles. But there must have been a smudge of mousse on my glasses, because I accidentally read it as "35 miles," then set the device down and went back to sight-seeing. We had probably muted the phone for Mass, so the usual GPS digital voice announcing "Recalculating!! Recalculating!" was not heard. If ignorance is bliss, I was indeed euphoric as we proceeded to get really lost!

In the hour or so that we went off track, at one point we got into a conversation about how odd it felt to be priests and not be at our parishes on the Lord's Day. Then we started noticing the number of young adults in the streets of the towns. When we drove past a church, the age of the people coming out or heading in were very much like our parish churches. Of a mature age....you know, statistically senior!

One of us wondered aloud how many of these twenty-something French folk had been out socializing the night before. Dance music and the beat we called disco has lived on in many European countries longer than even Donna Summer could hold a note at the height of America's disco craze. In an inspired moment, Fr. Joseph said "They still seem to have 'Saturday Night Fever.' It's too bad we can't get them to catch Sunday Morning Fever!" We had a good laugh at the irony, and then he suddenly exclaimed "Hey---why don't you write a disco song for your next album?!"

My first response was that he had put too much chocolate mousse over his oatmeal that morning, but then suddenly, the idea made a lot more sense. I quickly reached for my backpack, pulled out my journal and pen, and started writing. And a song was born. With my best recollection of polyester proms and Bee Gees beats, the lyric was finished in about ten minutes.

If the beat of the drum and the bass makes you dance...
don't forget who made your heart, give the good Lord a chance.
You can't see who you are...in that mirrored disco ball
It just spins you around, so hear the church bells that call!!

I need, you need, a Sunday Morning Fever
I say, the Lord's day is meant for all believers
So don't say you're too cool in your "disco inferno"
'cause the Lord of the Dance gives joyful life eternal...

When the fever of Saturday night starts breaking
There's a place for your face in God's House, it's there for the taking...

Don't dance with your deceiver, catch Sunday Morning Fever
All holiness achievers have Sunday Morning Fever...
Even Wally and the Beaver had Sunday Morning Fever!

I need, you need, a Sunday Morning Fever......

When the time came to record my next album, the disco song was an obvious choice. From the middle of the road, my music was suddenly hijacked into the middle of the dance floor. I could hardly sing it without laughing. There's even a little musical bridge where I do a rather pathetic falsetto Bee Gee imitation. The background vocals by Mary Rozak and Mary Beth Harper added a hilarious parody quality that we may never reach—or, for that matter, ever attempt again.

An extremely low-budget music video was shot on what couldn't even be called a shoestring budget, because I was wearing penny loafers. It included an opening sequence that blatantly stole from the *Saturday Night Fever* scene of John Travolta's feet, strutting to the hypnotic beat of disco at its best. Instead, I and my loafers are walking up the aisle of Blessed Sacrament church. If the description tongue-in-cheek fits our attempt at musical parody, then tongue-through-cheek would adequately fit the video. It was up-loaded to YouTube.com with the hopes of going "viral" selling lots of CDs and even more importantly, getting a few laughs while still making a serious point about church attendance. Unorthodox, for sure! But I knew from my film and comedy writing years that you sometimes have to paint with broad strokes to get a point across.

What I quickly discovered in my early donations to cyberspace media outlets is that not everybody has the same sense of humor. While friends, family, parishioners, and a number of strangers clicked on my video link and posted positive comments, there were a few others who were not as kind. One very traditional Latin Mass promoting website posted my video as an example of "blasphemy," while another internet video critic said "It's priests like you that are chasing people out of the Catholic Church."

After the initial shock wore off, I concluded that I'm in the best of company, for Jesus Christ also was accused of blasphemy. And, in my experience, He has a great sense of humor. Others may not, but they deserve our pity. I guess you can lead a horse to water, but you can't make him participate in a Gallop Poll.

Wishin' on the first star, dreaming in the dark
Workin' for a living wond'rin' if I'll leave a mark
Baby-steps as tiny as an ant in Central Park..
But I'm walkin' in the footprints of God!

The Conversion of a Frown

❧ ❧ ❧ ❧ ❧ ❧ ❧

I'm waiting for the day when what I fry won't stick
Like the ad says, special coating makes it slide
Sure, you're waiting also, Lord, for your Gospel to take root
When the great things I've been taught will be applied
I'll butter up my foolish pride, let your saving truth inside.

Mercy---marinate my heart, toss all my cares upon the grill
Love, like a holy grease of grace
cooks disappointments into thrills
Don't let my feelings burn, flip my burgers 'til golden brown
For what's at stake in the bar- b-cue
Is the conversion of a frown!

Yes, I'm looking toward the day when what I say comes to be
When the promises to God I truly do…
But, you're patient with me, Lord,
til the creed will fit my need
And a thread of hope to needle's eye comes through…
'til I stick like super glue, to all I vowed to you…

C'mon, Jesus, reverse my frown, upside down
We can really go to town, and give glory to your crown!

Chapter Eleven

THE CONVERSION OF A FROWN

One of the most challenging fields of work I attempted in my vocation search involved working as a portrait photographer for Buffalo's part of a national chain of photography studios. It was the job I took after almost a decade as a professional file clerk. Partly, because after five years of desperate searching, it was the *only* full-time job that I was offered by anyone but God (whose voice I was ignoring with my own litany of dreams.)

After accepting the position, I rejoiced that my fingers would no longer be smudged like an Ash Wednesday forehead every Sunday afternoon by pouring through the Want Ads for work. My tender Irish skin would finally be safe from legions of paper cuts and staple bites from handling mountains of medical records. However, I could not have foreseen the sign of the cross, the dying inside that I would eventually face by becoming part of this system.

I thoroughly enjoyed the chance to work with people. File folders have their purpose, but they hardly ever contribute to conversation except for a few symbolic gestures through deep cuts and the occasional lacerations. I can still vividly recall reaching toward a shelf of file folders and the sensation of a stray edge of a manila folder slicing part of my hand. The company that hired me offered a wide variety of photographic subjects: baby portraits, children of all ages, couple engagement photos, whole-family portraiture, and even, for the first few months of my employment, pet sittings! (The area management had the option to cease including Fido and Boo-Boo Kitty, and rumor had it that one squeak of dog toy too many—without giving it to the drooling animal-- caused one of my co-workers to get bitten.)

After about six weeks of training, working alongside an experienced photographer, I learned the formula of the company. There were exact and specific poses, down to the angle of the head turn, the body posture and where their eyes should be looking. I learned what to avoid in group shots, such as the "totem pole," where the person behind would appear to have his head piled on top of the one in front. In some cultures, this was considered traditional, but in this company it was a huge no-no. When the proofs came back from the factory, you could lose points on your evaluation and get the sense that heads would roll if heads were lined up too much like a Native American artifact. And no smoking of a peace pipe could reverse that.

I actually had only a few years of amateur photo experience at the time. My investment in my first 35mm camera and subscription to a photography magazine sent me off in a fantasy that I could do *that* for a living. When my first nephew and godchild, Kevin Patrick was born, I was personally responsible for keeping Kodak as well as Fotomat (remember those little islands of film development??) in the black. Kevin was the first grandchild to two large families, and we often say his feet didn't touch the ground for about three years. Everybody waited in line for their chance to hold the baby. I took my turn, but also spent a great deal of time focusing, framing and shooting miles of film. My family said he might eventually hold me liable for the retina burn from all those flashes of light, so after a while, I took outdoor photos in natural light and just kept shooting. He was a great subject and smiled easily in response to my faces. Or was he laughing at me? Hmmmm....

At the portrait studio newborn babies were placed in a special chair with a layer of foam rubber that had a little egg-shaped divot where you could "sit" the baby even when they were too young to hold their heads up. The company's formula was worked out very precisely, and I even learned how to do a double exposure where the child's face was glancing toward the light and at the same time, looking adorably toward the camera. The idea was to get the cutest poses and expressions so that parents and grandparents would buy many prints.

The sales aspect of the job always felt kind of phony to me. You were supposed to say "Oh—these are going to be gorgeous!!" "I can't wait to see that shot. It might be perfect as a 20 X 24 canvas for the grandparents!" Sometimes, my inner voice was saying "So glad my parents never did this to us! Some kids get better looking when they grow up. Don't feel bad, kid. " But on the outside, I was trained to act as if I had never seen such a child. And that if they didn't buy enlargements, I might just have to purchase some myself. Even though these were strangers' children. And...most of them were cute, but not the kind of cute the Disney channel builds a television series and recording career around.

The Christmas-lover in me was delighted that I was instructed to start doing portraits with holiday-themed backgrounds in October. That would allow the customers to get their order to the North Pole's Portrait Elves for air brushing and massive printings. The company would offer "free" coupons for an 8x10 in women's magazines as a gimmick to get them to call for a sitting appointment. Then we were supposed to try to sell them enough copies in enlargements and wallet sizes to drop as leaflets over Chicago, Tokyo or New York City on Christmas Eve. Admittedly, my photography work was pretty darn good most of the time. I still have a small pile of proofs that I saved for my portfolio of infants who were really beautiful babies looking like angels. And, I must admit, I saved a few of the ones whose expressions looked as if I were trying to get them to smile by holding a rattle snake up to their faces. Just for the record, I never did that. But one secret of photographing a four-to-six-month old is that you can simply smile at them and say "Ahhh-boo!" But that stops working at about eight months where the "boo" part makes them shriek and hide behind their mother. Experience is a great teacher!!

I also saved some of the unusual proofs from the adults or family group portraits. For the big groups, there was a need to be somewhat schizophrenic in approach. My ability to act silly to get a smile from different age groups had to include my Kermit the Frog voice (complete with puppet!) as well as rattle shaking for infants. For the grown-ups, I'd put on my best stand-up comedy routine to warm them up while I was positioning them. "Head down, turn this way….chin to the left, lean back, lean up…and doesn't *that* feel natural?? Of *course* not," I'd say with a smile, and they'd usually smile in response. And---flash! Got it!

Toddlers who'd been fed, burped, napped, and diaper changed at biologically appropriate times were almost always an easy sitting. Sometimes you just had to say their names, and they smiled. I would marvel at how easy it could be, then say to myself "Wow—they're paying me five dollars an hour for this??" (My hourly rate after priestly ordination would be considerably less…but the benefits are eternal, I hope)! Other kids without the best-case scenario of diaper care, gas, and hunger would arrive "not in a good space", as we say, or simply become traumatically terrified by the nice man in the shirt and tie with the puppet on his hand. I can't say that I blame them, because, honestly, who hasn't at one time or another had a fear of clowns? Bozophobia un-treated can lead to a three-ring circus of irrational anxieties. While there was no clown make-up or fright wig in front of these kids, perhaps something as simple as the size of my shoes gave them the notion. It's not *my fault* I that have big feet.

Only once in my eternal twelve months of working there did I lose my patience with a parent. It was a valuable life lesson in the fact that some people don't listen nor do they follow directions, even ones that are announced, then repeated like the life boat drill at the launch of the *Titanic*. Kids who were old enough to sit up would be placed on a table that was covered by a furry cloth that resembled carpeting by the Muppets. My instruction was very careful and clear to the parent (usually a mother) that they were to sit right next to the child with their hand firmly holding the back of their shirt or dress. Their hand or arm would not be in the shot from the angle that I was using. Under no circumstances were they to let go of the child's shirt or coat until I told them to. And they were not to move from their seat or let go, or speak to little Glinda while I was trying to get them to look in a certain direction, or every picture would be a profile. Mom's voice will always draw them. For the next ten minutes, they need to follow my voice.

It was difficult at times to convince parents that someone besides themselves could ever produce a smile on their kid's face, or at the very least (after ten minutes of pleading, toy-squeaking and uttering silly words) what would pass for a pleasant expression. Too big a smile can actually ruin a portrait as well, for squinting closes the eyes and decreases the face value in a professional portrait. Of the thousands of mothers I worked with, only one broke the commandment about her always holding on, and her child careened off the table onto the floor.

I completely lost it with this woman. Maybe it was the fact that the company who employed me grossly over-scheduled certain hours of the day. More than likely it was the fact that she ignored my safety instructions and greatly endangered her little girl. Suffice it to say that I was grateful that the child was not seriously injured, and that I did not injure the mother for her stupidity. My faith in guardian angels got stronger, even though my face stayed bright red for the next two or three sittings; and my heart, when it finally started beating again, was palpitating with a panic pattern.

After the Christmas rush, the second-most busy portrait season was Spring, for the Buffalo area's heavily-Catholic population included hundreds of children whom we could photograph for their First Holy Communion. I loved these sessions, because although I could certainly have been fired for doing so, I would do some evangelization as I worked. The white communion dresses against a black background made the girls look so sweet, the boys in dark suits against the white screen…I sometimes wondered if I could freelance for *Tiger Beat* if they ever did a celebrity First Communion special edition.

What I found, to my dismay, was that very often the parents would carry in a small bible and rosary beads. They'd hand them to me for use as "props," and as I positioned their hands holding the bible or folded them piously, I would casually say. "Do you know how to pray the rosary? I love the rosary!" and "Make sure you read this bible, it's not just a prop!" The company's owners probably could have given me a pink slip on the spot, but it was much more interesting and exciting to talk about sacraments and devotions than to pose them for a picture. Signs of more to come, as I now know. For almost twenty years, I've had the privilege of giving children their First Eucharist. And most parishes have a no-photo policy during that solemn moment. A photographer is often hired to take pictures afterwards, and I cannot explain the euphoria that I feel when I realize that his/her duties are no longer mine!! However, when we line up the children for a group photo after Mass and we announce that the parents wait until after the professional photographer gets his shots, I do feel like I'm back in my photo studio days. Because after the announcement, about twenty of the parents/grandparents start snapping away. I guess it's hard to obey instructions when your darling child looks so sweet and holy.

Family portraits were sometimes a greater challenge, but I now realize that preaching to a church full of people on Christmas and Easter is what the Lord was teaching me. A family photo would often include up to 35 people of various ages, grandparents, their children and grandchildren, and occasionally the family pet! I had to convince them that this photo would be an heirloom for generations to come, but only if they purchased a copy for each person in the group and anyone else who ever knew them. Especially if the adults cooperated and tried to look happy, or even if they were faking it.

The worst experience of this type of chaos was a family who filled my little studio in Depew, New York. I spent about ten feverish minutes lining them up by height, arranging for some of them to stand on little wooden boxes so that there would be good geometric shapes among the heads to please my supervisors, and figuring out a way to get children in every imaginable age group to look at me and smile on cue.

I had to be an octopus of activity after they were in place, with a puppet on one hand, a facial tissue to brush across the baby's chin to get a smile, and comments to entertain the teenagers enough to temporarily get the bored looks off their faces. Just about everyone was looking happy, in the direction of the camera. Then, I saw the ogre in the back row. He looked like a cousin they had brought in from the back woods, or some kind of island cult of wild men. With hair bushy and unruly, his facial expression as if I were offering to steal his motorcycle and call him a sissy in front of his friends in Hell's Angels.

I ran to the back of the group and got close to him, forcing a smile and whispering so only he could hear: "Help me out here, buddy. The kids are smiling, even the dog is smiling. You look like you lost your best friend. One little smile and we can both can get out of here!" I stepped back with my camera's trigger switch in hand, took a breath, and with the rehearsed line "Say Moneeeeeeey," squeaked a toy, waved Kermit in a circular motion, and quickly shot a few pictures.

But the cave man won. Stone Age and stone face. A week or two later, Shirley, my Proof Consultant, met with members of the clan. She pointed out how darling all the kids looked, she gave me credit for getting a Rottweiler to grin. But we didn't sell a thing, after I had sweated off about five pounds in desperation. Mr. Cranky-Pants was all they could see. Deep down, I knew this work wasn't my calling. But occasionally in my ministry as a priest I can go back to those days and arrange a family at a 50th wedding anniversary Mass like a pro. And it's a relief to not have to worry about selling them copies of the photos. It's a joy to just capture the moment. And if I'm invited into the picture, you can believe I follow whatever the photographer says. I just have to be careful not to grab the back of the shirt of the person standing next to me. They always take that they wrong way....

Camera Candids

My first exposure to photography was the family's camera, my parents' actually, an inexpensive one with easily-installed film cartridges. I don't remember the moment when an opportunity arose to shoot a picture of anything but family birthdays, First Communions and other posed shots of people looking fairly uncomfortable. But somewhere in my mid-teens, I acquired my own camera on my birthday, and I instamatically became the creative director of an imaginary production company. In a flash, you could say, I was sold on the art form!

Recalling the square black and white photos of us as kids with the scalloped edges, wincing in the sun in the back yard pool, squinting in the light of the flash for indoor shots, something in me was determined to capture different perspectives. And maybe get a picture or two where our eyes were open! Candid photography as an artistic expression is very different from just lining the six Quinlivan kids up on the stairway off our living room in birth order. While those historic icons are valuable to us to this day (and recently, when our former home went up for sale, a few of us went to the Open House and did another stair pose, undoubtedly freaking out the realtor) a captured classic moment on film is an elusive treasure. How many times a blink can ruin a group shot, a sudden movement creates an un-wanted blur. These days, getting people to look up from their smart phones can be a major challenge.

My facial expression in childhood pictures, in all but the serious hand-folded Confirmation images when my sister Eileen and I received the sacrament the same night- could best be described as high-impact smiling. Eyes practically squeezed shut, vigorously trying to show all of my teeth as if the dentist had just begun an examination, it was not flattering in the least. My poor parents probably wanted to hang a Mona Lisa in my room for rehearsal of a less-hyper expression, to temper my exuberance before the camera. Later in life, I matured to modify that so that when we could afford color film processing, there would be a chance that you could actually detect my eye color.

Somehow, I quickly became the family photographer. I cannot recall anyone in particular taking that role before. It was kind of like a pick-up baseball game. "Somebody take a picture" became "Bill, get your camera!" Without formal training in this artform (fittingly, the same way I took up piano and guitar...) I learned by experimentation. Before I knew it, my eye could approximate the distance between the cheesy little plastic view-finder in the old cameras and the actual shutter. That would be the main factor in the common practice of pictorial decapitation, and was probably in the instruction pamphlet. The popular notion that men don't read directions is true in this case. Besides, the TV commercials always claimed you "just aim and shoot." What they didn't tell you was that you could shoot your Grandmother right out of the picture if you weren't careful. And, with that, you could surely get written out of her will.

Somewhere I still have the results of my first roll of film; candid shots of my sister Mary, wrapped in an orange and brown knitted afghan blanket, sitting in one of our fleet of rocking chairs, head-phoned in 1970's pop--or was it bubblegum-- bliss. My sister Sue on the telephone in her teenage years posed with an expression that she had just got through to a radio station and won Paul Anka concert tickets, and Eileen in braces, displaying a cake that she had just baked. As I recall, she's wearing a sweater with a knitted image of an apple across the front. (Who knew how prophetic that photo would be, as she would eventually major in Computer Science...but *not* work for Apple computers). My eldest brother Patrick successfully evaded my camera most of the time, but I recall a vivid image of my young brother Joe posing as if to be picking his nose. Humor runs through our family tree like Cazenovia Creek after a Spring thaw.

At some point in my vocational discernment, I decided to enter the world of SLR (single-lens reflex) cameras where the image you saw through the viewfinder was at least framed as it should appear on film. With that came adjustable focus and manually adjusted shutter speed and aperture. I began to read photography magazines and entered the exciting and frustrating world of the non-automatic. A skilled photographer (or, in my case, a lucky guesser) could create all kinds of visual images by adjusting the amount of light or the speed of the shutter. This meant that blurry, out-of-focus pictures could now be caused by many more reasons that the sudden movement of your subject!

Experimentation was fun and, as I said, frustrating. If I were trying to catch a bird in flight and hoped for a full wing span portrait, I could most often get either blurry birds or catch the moment when the wings were gathered inward instead of the soaring posture. Digital cameras of today do so much more to let you see within seconds that your photo is a success or failure. In those days, you would drop off your film at a drug store, and have to wait several days to see your work. Sometimes, the 36 exposures were all printed, and you could sort out the three or four shots you wanted to show people. Other times, the developers would choose not even to print shots that were so bad that they knew even their photographer wouldn't find redeeming value. Aren't you glad that our Creator doesn't do that??

Over the past thirty years or so, I've come to have greater respect for the visual arts because I know that my technical skills are based mostly on guessing. If we look at our relationship with God and prayer life as an album of snapshots, we might better assess our contribution to the art of faith. Who wouldn't want to learn to understand the importance of focus, framing, light, and such in our spiritual life? God does not seem to be offended by our guestimation and approximation, for we're dealing here with divine mystery, and it's never as simple as what we capture on film. So often, it's the soul's inner lens that sees, and no device has been invented that can display our experiences of the deep soul on a screen, to be processed and printed on photo paper. Yet, our God-moments leave indelible images on our hearts, in our memories.

About a decade ago, before embarking on a pilgrimage to Rome and Assisi, I bought a small tripod for my digital camera. Gradually, I'd grown discouraged by the different timing of the digital format; there's a moment of delay between releasing the shutter button and the actual photograph being taken as compared to the quicker, more instant response of SLR photography. The threat of blurry pictures continued to hang over me, as some once-in-a-lifetime moments were ruined by movement, and automatic elements that my higher-tech digital camera made decisions for me. Automation can steal an artist's creative moment.

One photo opportunity in St. Peter's Basilica in Rome stands out as this photographer's graced moment of clarity. From the tiny windows in the dome, a shaft of sunlight was breaking through and cascading down to the marble floor. It was breath-taking and inspiring, and every pilgrim in our group reached for their cameras to start shooting. I, sensing that this could be a make-or-break moment of confidence-building (or shattering) quickly attached my new mini tripod to my camera. I backed up and headed toward a rather large area of the marble floor where there was no crowd at that moment. I zoomed out wide to capture a floor-to ceiling (earth to Heaven) view. I adjusted the tripod so the camera head was pointed up, studied the viewfinder, then held my breath and gently pushed the shutter.

The resulting photograph is one of the best I've ever taken. Its beauty actually moves me to re-phrase that; the photo was "taken" but the reality of the awesome beauty in sight was *given*. Being on holy ground, hoping to capture what my eyes could see, I experienced a moment of blessing in God's presence. When my friend Wendy's boys were young she used to teach them that the rays of awesome light that break through the clouds and seem to spread like fingers in a hand from eternity are "God rays." In St. Peters, on a lovely, sunny Italian morning, I was touched by those shafts of holy light. All the elements of photography came together, and the Creator and the created were in communion. That experience I carry in my heart as much as the printed photo in my album as an interior snap-shot of the holy.

What is it about certain moments that we want to immortalize or hold onto in film or photography? Our minds have a capacity to file those sights and sounds, but we long to keep these experiences in a form that we can frame, enlarge, and share. On a vacation with my sister Mary and some friends, we flew to Los Angeles, then rented a car and drove to Salt Lake City, Utah, and flew home from there. While I shot a lot of film in Hollywood- the stars on the Walk of Fame that I liked, places on movie studio back lot tours like the *Leave it to Beaver* house exterior, and amazing colors in the deserts of Nevada- a ten-minute cable car ride was one of my most memorable thrills.

Somewhere in Utah's Rockies, we stopped at a place where you could take a ride up the side of a mountain. Mary wasn't keen on heights, but I was psyched, and loaded up my old 35mm Canon camera with 36 exposures of 100 speed film. Our friends Ann Marie Poulter and Kris Samel were also photo buffs, so we paid the fee and stepped into the vehicle. The first thing that struck me as we smoothly glided upward was the glass floor through which you could see straight down to the ground. While I had never had any motion sickness on amusement park rides, I took a glance down and discovered for a moment what the fear of falling could be. From that moment on, I just kept looking out and up. And therefore, my breakfast stayed put.

Riding up the mountain, I could not believe the majesty before my eyes. The pine trees and greenery on the sides were spectacular, the enormous reach of these earthly chunks of creation were instantly awe-inspiring. Of course, the fact that we didn't have to climb was certainly a bonus. Mountain-climbing as a sport had never occurred to me, coming from Buffalo where our mountains were made by snow plows and melted away each Spring. But in these few moments, I knew that I could ride up mountains for the rest of my life and never be bored! The Biblical experiences of Moses and other key persons meeting God on mountaintops made perfect sense as my heart was filled with a fresh jubilation and view of creation. From that cable car, we also had an awesome perspective of the other mountains, and I shot all 36 photos of my roll of film in rapid succession.

I couldn't wait to get the pictures developed and was not disappointed other than the fact that an 8x10 enlargement seemed quite puny. I soon realized that even a mountain-sized poster would not actually re-create the thrill of the actual sight, or the joy of the ride. But I was satisfied with the focus and framing for once. And the sight of that framed mountain shot hanging in my rectory room still brings me back in spirit to that day when every time I look at the photograph. Apparently, that's why we shoot pictures. A glimpse of awesome is always better than nothing at all.

Have you ever wondered what God's favorite "Kodak moment" with you and me might be? Certainly, the Lord who created the inventors of the instruments that we use to record what we see has some beyond-highest-tech form of record-keeping and unlimited memory!! To me, God has to have a perfect scrapbook of moments, days and years of our lives that give Him joy. Or maybe some of us will be given the task of filing and reviewing those things once the live-action and earthly life has ended. Hmmmm….I might just volunteer for that project in the Kingdom! Perfect focus, lighting provided by the one who said "Let there be light…" it's got to be beyond what my camera's eye and my own mind can see. And I have almost ten years' experience as a file clerk. Who knows how that will come in handy in Heaven.

Chapter Twelve

HUMBLE PIES ARE SQUARED

I seriously don't know how the Pharisees and Sadducees got so full of themselves. They obviously needed the ego balloon deflated and Jesus had the perfect pin to pop it. I find that my daily life as a priest keeps me constantly aware that this isn't about me. As soon as I start to believe that illusion, I'm brought back to reality, thank God. On the one hand, it's easy to see how I can get in the way of the message at times, but in other ways, God's providence includes many servings of humble pie. A few of them take the cake!

As a non-memorizer, I have to concentrate very hard when reading from the liturgical books, especially now that I have bifocals. One moment of looking out into the congregation too long and I can easily say "I have not come to serve but to be served" and turn the Gospel into the opposite of what it means. I once heard that a priest accidentally said during the consecration: "He took the cup, broke it, gave it to his disciples and said: take this, all of you and eat it…" One word makes a difference, and its' easier to break and eat bread, though I cannot speak from experience regarding breaking and eating a cup. Thank God the recent translation now says *chalice*. It's less a household word and has to decrease the threat of malapropism in a moment of decreased concentration or distraction.

My mother, who like all moms had an especially potent worry gene, once told me as I was entering seminary that I should really start to learn more about sports so that I could pretend to have something in common with the people who were mad about them. What I've found in following that advice is that I spend more time in shame's penalty box for half-hearted attempts at sportiness. Of course, I do know the basics of major league sports, but it's easier to claim to know nothing so that expectations are lowered. The few times I've tried to appear on the cutting edge of pro sports, I've learned that integrity sacrificed for alleged coolness just makes a bigger fool in the end. Or is it the end zone??

Strangely, during all four years of seminary education, the Buffalo Bills (an NFL football team, for those of you who are like me, and have reason to pretend to know) miraculously made it to the Super Bowl every year of my theological studies. As one of my duties of service to the seminary community I was co-manager of the soda bar in the recreation building, so I had to host the Super Bowl parties. Actually, I had heard so much football talk that I could actually recognize the names of several of the players. I would latch on to gridiron terms and try to use them.

For example, they can kick the ball for an "extra point" also known as a conversion. So after the kicker would make the football go through the posts, I'd say to the priest or seminarian next to me: "I've been praying for his conversion!" That kind of comment didn't get me invited to ESPN's SportsCenter as a guest host, and for that I am eternally grateful. I've been on EWTN, and that was a much better fit and a task much easier to tackle.

A few years later, I was preaching at a Penance service for about 150 high school teens in St. Gregory's Confirmation program. The scripture I chose to illustrate the Lord's great mercy was the Isaiah prophecy "a bruised reed he will not break, a smoldering wick he will not quench." When preparing my homily, I had a flash-back to Mom's well-intended advice that I try harder to know about sports, so it came to me that 'bruised reed' sounded like one of the Buffalo Bills. So I stood there, with false bravado saying "It's like that guy who plays for the Bills... Bruce Reed. The *bruised reed* he will not break...." The kids just looked at me like teenagers often do...blank and expressionless, but with an added expression of confusion. Afterwards, Fr. Jim Bastian told me that the players are named Bruce Smith and Andre Reed. For an instant I entertained the thought that some of them didn't know the Bills players. So....now, it's I who's confused. And I didn't have to pretend about that!

As a songwriter, sometimes I am overly sensitive to the feedback I get from my original compositions. Probably, I could polish them up a bit more before singing them the first time in public, but on some special occasions I get an idea for a song so close to the event, that there's a short turn-around time to the completion deadline. One such case was the dedication of the new parish church at St. Mary of the Lake in Hamburg where I served as a seminarian, then as transitional deacon, and then for my first year of priesthood. I lived in the parish during the years of fund-raising and planning for a new worship space.

They had been using a little brick building that was fine in the 1940's, but the parish had very much outgrown it. For a priest, a first assignment is comparable to a honeymoon. People are very kind and forgiving to the newly-ordained, though they sometimes share awkward thoughts like: "You just look so cute up there in those vestments...like a little kid playing priest!" St. Mary's parishioners are great folks, and having contributed to the building fund myself over several years and visiting the construction site from time to time, I definitely looked forward to being at its dedication. I also had an idea for a special song for the occasion, and it seemed to come together pretty quickly in the writing process.

At last, the day of our new church building's dedication came, and it was a delightful celebration. I had offered to share my new song, and they graciously scheduled it as a post-communion meditation. Excited, nervous, and a little bit emotional being back where I first served as a rookie priest, I sat at the piano and sang *"Living Word, Living Bread."* I can't remember if I made my usual announcement that my desire was to offer the song as music ministry, so I prefer that people not applaud as if at a concert performance. Honestly, I have no recollection of whether they applauded at the end, or took a moment of silent prayer, which I like to say is the most appropriate response to an offered prayer other than "Amen!"

What I remember most clearly is that after all the priests processed into the vestibule after Mass, a monsignor many years my senior turned to me and blurted: "Your song sounded like '*Red River Valley*'" I stopped, like a freight train had suddenly crossed in front of me at the railroad tracks on Rogers Road. One of my greatest fears as a beginning songwriter was that my tunes would be derivative; that is, sound so much like another song that it would appear that I had borrowed another's melody. While I dearly love writing song parodies and used to like making a high school classmate laugh until he fell off his chair with lyrics from pop songs I'd re-write to roast the teachers- this stung to the heart.

Honestly, in that moment I had no idea what *"Red River Valley"* sounded like, but I vaguely recalled that it was an old country and western/cowboy movie song. And the old priest who said it had a tone that the world would later come to recognize as the voice of singing competition judge Simon Cowell... on a day that he'd just heard that his cat died. No matter how many of my little church ladies and other friends commented positively that day, I had sunken into a valley red with embarrassment and humiliation. I would, of course, get over it, eventually seeing it as something to humble me. Please pass the pie, Lord.

At other times, when I sing at a church gathering, people will approach me with feedback that tries to compare me to successful, professional music-makers. But their analogies are all over the musical map. A very nice man who attended a day of retreat that I led told me that "When you play piano and sing, you remind me of...Barry Manilow!!" Now, don't get me wrong, I love Barry's music. It's in my iPod and I actually have many of his songs almost memorized. (For as much as my brain can memorize, so that's saying a lot). But after the comment, I had to ask, gingerly, "and so...you *like* Barry Manilow, right???"

Once, when doing music ministry for a priest retreat with Sr. Briege and Fr. Kevin in Sioux Falls, South Dakota, a priest came to me at the end of the week and told me that my singing reminded him of Robert Goulet. "Wow-I wondered---what happened to Barry Manilow?" And then, how do I take that, when in my youth I only knew Robert Goulet for three things: first, he was married to the beautiful Carol Lawrence, secondly, he sang mostly in Vegas lounges, and third, legend has it that once Elvis Presley saw him singing on a TV program and shot out the screen with a revolver. Obviously, sometimes Elvis doesn't leave the building but invites YOU to!

I was again relieved to hear that Robert Goulet was one of this priest's favorite singers. Gosh, it's hard to take a compliment when the comparison is to someone who seems to be so different from oneself. So now I practice humbling myself regarding my music before others can surprise me.

When I play guitar and unconsciously swing the neck of the instrument in vertical motions, I try to prepare myself for the inevitable comment: "Hey---you play guitar just like Danny Partridge!!" And I hum to myself... c'mon, get humble....

The cover photo on my first CD shows me standing in a field of green, arms open wide and smiling upward. *Paintbrush in the Green* actually has a technology-enhanced secret. The original photo, shot by Cathy Bohan during a tour of Ireland, was in black and white! In the beautiful picture she took, I'm wearing a black sweatshirt. So we photo-shopped a tiny white square up near my collar to make me look like a priest. I also had my 35mm camera in my right hand, so an artist digitally removed my right hand---I didn't feel a thing!--- duplicated and reversed my left hand and inserted it where the camera used to be. When I divulge this fact, I always say that some people claim to have two left feet, but I can truly say that I have two left hands! And the left hand never lets the other left hand know what it's doing...

It's one kind of experience to sell your music on CD or through online downloads. It's another to give them away. When the *Priest of Mine* project came out in the Year of the Priest, 2009, I decided to give them at no charge to priests I'd meet during that special year. After all, the songs had been given to me; why not share? I found that giving them was a joy but my wacked-out insecurity could quickly surface. Especially if I asked an ordained clergyman "Would you like a copy of my CD?" and there was a pause. The few seconds of awkward silence could merely be their mind calculating how much cash they have in their wallet, if they initially thought I was trying to make a sale. But to me I couldn't help wonder if they were trying to think of a polite way to say "No thanks. I'm allergic to singing priests." Or, "I gave you up for Lent."

In Ireland and France, the CD give-aways were easiest. Priests on retreat are usually in a very good, kind, accepting mood. And I found that it's much easier to approach a stranger that you may never see again. The priests from Uganda and Brazil were especially excited to have one. In the back of my mind, I thought that they might just need a new coaster for their coffee mugs. The compact disc can also serve as a taper candle-holder, a very large earring or one of those special cones that the veterinarian puts on a pet's head to keep them from licking their stitches. It would have to be a *very* small pet. A lizard, maybe. I don't know any people or priests with pet lizards. But most of us have some pet peeves. Like run-on jokes that seem to never end a paragraph... okay... there... now it's done!

Joseph's Tears

❧ ❧ ❧ ❧ ❧ ❧

Wash us, O Lord, in Joseph's tears…
See God write an icon, of freedom from our lies
And we are saved, sanctified for ministry in Christ
Expiated by His death,
now our prayers like incense rise

Chapter Thirteen

JOSEPH'S TEARS

For forty days each year, Catholics journey spiritually through a season of Lent. In one sense, it's a type of Spring Training for the soul if you will allow a sports metaphor from someone who thinks a football is a prom for podiatrists. As the baseball players practice intently in warm Southern climates, some of us are still braving the chilly breezes of winter, chipping ice off our windshields, and melting it off our eyelashes. What both have in common is the goal of getting better at what we do, more focused on the playbook, listening to our "coach" and sliding into home. One can probably hit an occasional "home run" in Lent, but if you're going to experience a spiritual transformation it's a pilgrimage, uphill, into the wind, and it's more effective to brave the slippery surfaces than the well-worn paths. Nobody else on the team can bring about a Grand Slam but the Almighty!

One year as Lent approached, I was wondering how I could take the plunge deeper into the season's invitation to spiritual renewal. Picking up a Catholic periodical, I found an article about the long-lost art of letter writing as a spiritual exercise as well as a way of personal communication. The author shared that she hand-wrote letters to 40 people each Lent as a way to keep her connected to friends and family and to assure them of her prayers in the holy season.

What a treasure to come across this idea—my mind flashed back to my correspondence with Fr. John Kilian during his Maryknoll mission days. At the moment I read the article, I had just recently finished sending Christmas thank-you notes to parishioners for their generous, thoughtful gifts. But this concept now offered a new, more prayerful yet practical way to keep in touch. And beyond a basic "hope you're having a great Lent" wish, I got very excited about the challenge to write and share something going on in my life and ministry. It was very easy to come up with forty people, for my Christmas card list had about five times that number. Scanning the list, I decided to write to the people I would probably not encounter in person at this time of year; such as out-of-town friends and especially family. And this way, it had an element of surprise, for them as well as me! When I sat down to write, I enjoyed the time of personal out-reach as something that took me outside of myself.

Year one was a smash hit! I received several notes back from people, and one friend excitedly reported that she couldn't wait to try this herself the next year. When the next Lent came around, an idea surfaced that this practice could be a good exercise in building priestly fraternity. So, from the second year the focus switched to writing letters and notes to brother priests and the occasional bishop. I would write the note during my daily prayer time, and offer a special segment of intercessory prayer for the person who had been on my list for that day. The ordained ministers were quite responsive to a word of encouragement, and it helped me feel connected to them across the miles as we each served the people to whom we were assigned.

As with many things, I started the list of priests I'd write to in a familiar "comfort zone," choosing forty brothers whom I knew and wanted to contact; and for good measure, added a few whom I didn't particularly know well but admired for their ministry. That part of the list included priests who were prison chaplains, hospital chaplains, those who work in the Chancery offices, and a few of my seminary professors who were also ordained priests. At the annual Chrism Mass at St. Joseph's Cathedral on the Tuesday of Holy Week, I found that a number of priests who received the notes approached me and thanked me for my letters. Often they'd say something in the vein of "you'll never know how much I needed that affirmation/encouragement that day!" That night, the tradition at the Chrism Mass is for priests to renew their promises. Standing amid the vested concelebrants, I felt significantly more connected to them as well as appreciative of their gifts in the service of the Lord.

At the same time, my dear friend Fr. Joseph Bertha, a Byzantine Ruthenian Rite brother whose small parish was only a few blocks away from St. Gregory the Great, started sharing with me how the Eastern Rites of the Church celebrate Lent. It provoked me to examine my own sometimes too-easy routes like writing notes to the priests who I thought might appreciate my gesture. Fr. Joseph himself was following the practice of abstaining from meat for all of Great Lent (as they call it) and he had decided to offer that sacrifice to the Lord for the sake of priests whose vocations were in crisis.

He also loved the idea of writing letters to fellow priests, but he took the concept to another plane by reaching out to priests from his diocese who had left the ministry. (And he undoubtedly took it on *airplanes* as well---Fr. Joseph could be the poster child for Frequent Flyer Miles programs!) One Lent, he prayed for a particular brother and offered his fasting/abstaining for his sake. His letter shared that intention, as well as a direct invitation "I miss you at the altar of the Lord, and I invite you to come back!" On Good Friday, a phone call came. The brother priest had received the note, and he was touched. He shared: "In the years I've been out of active priestly ministry, nobody else ever invited me to return. I want you to know that I recently met with the bishop and I'm back!!"

When my cell phone rang, I saw on the caller ID that it was Fr. Bertha. But I could hardly understand him because he was crying. "He's BACK, Bill! Wait 'til you hear what the Lord did in answer to my prayers!!" My friend and I were in awe of what a personal note and the power of prayer and fasting can do. That Easter, as many priests renewed their promises at the Chrism Mass, one in particular returned to his calling. It seems in our busyness of administrative duties in our churches, we sometimes overlook the opportunity to use invitation as evangelization. But I doubt that my Byzantine friend nor I will ever forget that particular Easter's joy!

Fr. Joseph has also long been associated with the Patriarch Joseph from the book of Genesis. You may know him as the chap with a multi-colored coat and a Broadway musical that tells his story. Fr. Bertha's take on the story is that Joseph is a "type" of Christ, a story of salvation, a redemptive narrative passage from slavery to freedom. And the delightful Webber/Rice musical misses one very important detail---Joseph's tears. Seven times in the many chapters of Genesis, Joseph weeps, not for himself but for his brothers who betrayed him, his father Jacob, and the chosen people.

"You need to write a song about Joseph's Tears," my Eastern Rite icon-loving friend challenged me one day. While something inside me immediately started listing a million excuses not to accept the challenge, the Holy Spirit and Fr. Joseph Bertha kept inviting me. Tears can be a sign of a cleansing repentance, as we priests sometimes witness when hearing confessions. And, though as men we might not like to think about it, we also need to weep for our sins and the transgressions of our brothers. Holy tears are not only an emotion, but an outward sign of a heart that's turning, melting, and changing. Jesus is the perfect priest...we are His, but we also need to stay on a path of ongoing conversion and repentance.

Then wash us, O Lord, in your own tears, we pray!
Healing rain that makes us whole again
Weeping eyes then come to see
In Christ the slave set free...

The more I pondered and prayed about it, a myriad of interpretations for human tears came before me. We tend to think of weeping as only associated with sorrow, tragedy and frustration; and it certainly can be that. But tears can have as many shades and colors as Joseph's coat! People cry for a whole host of reasons. Our hearts can be touched profoundly by beauty, and by someone else's kindness. Moreover, a sunset, a loving gesture, and prolonged laughter can also produce tears.

I very clearly remember one day early in my first year of seminary. I brought my prayer books into the dormitory chapel about a half hour before the morning Mass. As I sat in the silence, a wave of amazing joy welled up in me. This was something new and different, spiritual and profound. I had not gotten a great grade on a theology exam. It wasn't caused by news that there would be donuts at the refectory breakfast table. It was a holy joy—and a sudden awakening that I was **finally** where God wanted me to be. This long period of seeking had taken a lot of attention and effort. The years of resume duplication and re-writing, the frustration of being hired at new jobs only to find within a week or two that little voice in my heart saying "you don't belong here, either"

....was now resolved. While there had been moments of being overwhelmed by the years of study before me, that particular morning something new dawned. The years of detours and U-turns had made finding my way feel like a calling in itself. Once I got accepted into the program, we went right to work, and there was not time to stop and realize, or stop and savor the moment. I had FOUND the path... the place where I was supposed to be after all that searching...and tears flowed freely, as I felt a grace in my soul that God was smiling with me.

Back to Lent and the hand-written epistles: over several years, Fr. Joseph came to call them the "BQ Top 40," which the music lover in me found to be a fitting nick-name. I shortened it to the "BQ 40" because it wasn't meant to single out my "top" or "favorite" brother priests. In fact, in subsequent years, my desire was to keep increasing the challenge of the task and therefore the list-making would have to become more challenging with time. Because it was Lent, the element of sacrifice was part of the letter-writing that I kept my eye on. It got to the point where I tried to find 40 priests in our diocesan directory that I knew the least, and reach out to them with a note and a prayer.

Without question, my goal to raise the bar each Lent reached new heights the year I felt called to look through the list of priests in my diocese and find some (I honestly cannot remember if there were 40 total...) who I was pretty sure didn't like me. It was quite painful to my ego, therefore, spiritually helping me realize where I need to grow in love and forgiveness, the day before Ash Wednesday as I assembled the list. Talk about being humbled... it was like an examination of conscience, for I had to face the fact that I also didn't much care for these priests who for whatever reason acted as if they didn't care for me. Some of that could just be my misguided perception, but then there was also a good chance that they simply found me rather obnoxious. I realized that I had given some of them reason to think that I am a jerk. Holy Lenten journeys, Batman! The season of purgation was really becoming harder than ever. My Irish soul whispered to itself: "Hey….maybe this will be your most authentic Lent ever. Stop whining, start writing."

These forty notes took a lot longer to write for obvious reasons. How do you word the sentiment "Dear Father So-and-so, This year I'm writing to priests who might actually dislike or hate me. Guess what--you're on the list. And apparently, I'm on yours!!" It was truly agonizing, to be honest. But the practice became a genuine work of mercy, and quickly led to a more sincere prayer for my brother priest. Jesus never commanded that we like one another; He taught us to love one another. And loving the ones we don't like can be transforming and freeing. So I started many of the notes by acknowledging that we are not close friends or may not have a lot more in common than the fact that we're both ordained priests.

I then asked their forgiveness if there was ever anything I had said or done to hurt or offend them. The process was like giving birth…not to twins or triplets but to a litter of 40 hand-written letters! The practice of asking for forgiveness during those weeks also made my confessions more grace-filled, as well as the ministry of hearing confessions. You can't preach forgiveness well unless you practice it, and it's been said that Christians are supposed to be among the best forgivers in the world, or our witness to Jesus is weak, lame and superficial. I personally found that I did not preach or sing songs of mercy the same way after asking for it from my brothers. Indeed, it's a gift that keeps on giving!!

The interaction at the next few diocesan priest gatherings was different from other years. I sensed that Jesus had done much healing that year, for me as well as others. In some large social gatherings most of us gravitate toward those with whom we feel most comfortable. But while that brought about many blessings for me, we all know-even the most naïve among us - that not every story has a happy ending. There were, as in other years, a number of written responses with reciprocal offers to pray. And then there were a few of the kind that mystery writers call poison-pen letters. They felt the need to respond by giving positive affirmation that they did, in fact find me obnoxious and annoying. Be careful what box you open, Pandora—you might just let something out that isn't pretty.

I'm rarely found completely speechless, but when I find myself in that position, I've developed a practice of taking mail with a bitter, hurtful edge (sometimes, anonymous critics whose tone makes British music mogul Simon Cowell sound like Mary Poppins) and putting it in between the pages of my hardcover copy of St. Maria Faustina's Diary, **Divine Mercy In My Soul**. It's great to have the saints to turn to in our family of faith, for they pray for us in a place where everything is love, everything is glory, and forgiveness is finally complete. We still live on the side of eternity where there's always going to be further work to be done.

We are still works in progress. Our lives can be seen as drafting a love letter to God. It's good news that we still have chances to re-write, edit, and even seal that letter with tears...of repentance, joy, or whatever your tear ducts are singing at the moment.

So, send us, O Lord, the gift of holy tears, we pray
As we confess send bitterness far from our souls
May we come as brothers who are open and contrite
And, like Joseph, reconcile...in Mercy's multi-colored light.

Chapter Fourteen

GOD SPELLED BACKWARDS...

Almost every year, my letters to Santa Claus as a boy included a request for a puppy. Our next-door neighbors were single ladies and they always had dogs. They were generous and patient neighbors who recognized a kid desperate for a four-legged friend. I would stick my hand through the chain link fence and pet Mimi, the French poodle and Samantha, a black Labrador retriever. As the years passed, my hands out-grew that method, so I would watch from our front porch window for Mary Lou Fitzgerald to come home from the grocery store and then run out to help her carry in the bags. The ulterior motive was probably very obvious to her, but she never questioned me.

Yes, it was a poorly- veiled act of charity...kind of embarrassing to admit at this ripe old age, but it's true. After carrying in the grocery bags, Mimi and Sam would come to me for some attention and affection. And, then Mary Lou would open the box of dog treats (always on her shopping list and certainly a sure-fire magnet for canine fidelity) and let me give a treat to each one. Something very deep in my soul had that boy-and-his-dog connection, but my parents were not able to fulfill that dream.

141

In the intervening years, other friends who had dogs would let me share vicariously in the fun; walking and even bathing Cocoa, the Donohue's collie mix, and enjoying visits with family who had dogs. Why is Fr. Bill out in the garage? The dog is there!! My mother shared with me when I was older how she and my Dad would shake their heads at my perseverance in asking for a pup of my own. But the decision was made before I was born. And proper authority in the family meant that parents were really in charge. A dog simply wasn't in the cards.

My father had been a postman in his young adult life, all-too-often growled at, barked at, and chased by canine patrons who apparently didn't get their latest issue of Paws Illustrated on time, and they made their opinions known. Somehow, God didn't give pets the ability to understand the adage: don't blame the messenger… For some reason, Dad took this to mean that dogs didn't like him. And he let it be known in no uncertain terms that he didn't care for them. Like the parents and other adults in the film classic, *A Christmas Story* telling Ralphie "You'll shoot your eye out!" in response to dreaming of getting a BB gun for Christmas, Dad's standard response to my regular requests for a puppy was: "It'll bite the neighbors and I'll get sued." To my childish mind, it seemed worth the risk, and besides, a few of the neighbors could have used a little holy fear of the Lord (or dog spelled backwards) as well as some obedience training!

In July of 2009, having been a pastor for four years and finding that even Santa Claus had started to ignore my e-mails, faxes, and pleading letters, I decided that I might finally become a dog-owner. *Owner* sounds so impersonal, *master* sounds more commanding than I can be, so suffice it to say my dog dream became a reality. And I instantly discovered the reason that God spelled backward is dog. It's like holding a mirror up to unconditional love! Yes, I know that human beings are created in God's image and likeness. But He also made creatures for our delight, and dogs seem to have an ability to cross over from pet to friend and family member. You letter carriers out there can just skip to the next chapter. I learned long ago that puppy love is not in your vocabulary!

Now, I have been known in my life as a crazed Marie Osmond groupie, an Amy Grant fan, a Sound of Music/Mary Poppins aficionado, (yes-- of course, and a Jesus Freak... hopefully that will never change), as well as a Christmas music-obsessed violator to those who strictly observe Advent. But adopting a dog truly opened a new category of description that I could have not seen coming. Becoming a head-over-heels, over the brink, dog lover.... happened in an instant and was more than I had hoped for. And, I'll freely admit, a little scary in its heart-stealing aspects.

Dogs are always fascinating and often frustrating, but their reputation as "man's best friend" is really, really true. While I admit that I have received some very warm and affectionate receptions upon entering rooms in the first 49 years of this life, nothing compares to the enthusiastic exaltation of Benny, my West Highland Terrier, when I arrive. And if I have had the nerve to go on retreat or a few days of vacation, the production number of excessive jumping, running, and face-licking ratchets up exponentially. And that's just *my* jumping, running, etc. You should see how excited **Benny** gets!

My initiation into the Crazy Dog Lovers club was quick. I still have to try to temper my enthusiasm to introduce him to visitors and/or show strangers in line at the grocery store the latest pictures on my phone. My parents never invested in a home-movie camera, so hundreds of family and friends were spared film festivals of the 6 of us. But I have more than made up for that with movies of Ben at his best. My cell phone has video of him on Santa's lap at the pet store, recordings of him frolicking in the back yard snow, and squeaking a toy. When I recorded my voice mail message on the phone, Benny sat next to me and chewed a toy hot dog to accompany me with pet percussion.

Fr. John Aurelio, who was my spiritual director in seminary, loved dogs. He used to say that it was good for a priest to have another living thing to be responsible for, lest we become too centered on ourselves. In my pre-Benny era, I had plants, and actually had a few of them survive about ten years. They did fit the description of living things. As house plants, they were dependent on me for watering, opening the drapes for sunshine, I even performed a few successful pot transplants. But I found them very hard to walk on a leash, and the only tricks I could get them to do were "sit" and "stay". They wouldn't flower on command either. Not much fun, I had to conclude.

Dog ownership as an ordained minister has its ministry benefits. A priest walking his dog can be a stealth approach to neighborhood evangelization. When people with small children see Benny they get very excited. Who can blame them? The kids often ask "Can we pet your dog?", "What's his name?", and my favorite, "Where does he live?" I love that they never ask where I live, but I am nowhere nearly as cute as my dog, nor do I wag my tail excitedly or sit on command on the cold sidewalk. But in certain moments, if they held the right treat in their hand, say, a Hershey's kiss with almonds, I could be quite obedient!

On our walks, I explain that Benny lives with me, in the house at the Church. If he could talk, how I wish I could teach him to then say "If you'd like to register as a parishioner, I'll lick your Sunday envelopes!" In nice weather a number of people walk through our parish grounds, and often the dog and I are in the fenced-in back yard. Benny is glad to have visitors, though we have to watch that they don't give him treats. His allergies and other digestive restrictions mean that a careful eye has to be kept on what he eats. He suffers from allergy amnesia, too. If someone offers him a bacon-flavored bite of something, he tries to get it in his mouth before I can explain his dietary limits to them. I suspect that he writes to Santa Claus and asks for a secret delivery of Liver Snaps. He can't reach the mailbox, so I don't know how he'd get it mailed to the North Pole. But I do take him to the pet stores for a photo on Santa's lap. I wouldn't be surprised if he's whispering a list of edible Christmas gifts that he wants but isn't allowed to eat.

Have you ever wondered whether our obedience training as disciples wouldn't have a more lasting effect if we learned from our four-legged friends? Once a dog learns its name and knows his master's voice, face and scent, there's a bond that doesn't fade. The patience needed to get a puppy to understand a firm "no" when they venture into dangerous territory has to reflect in some small way the formation of our human conscience. Animals act mostly by instinct, and dogs have been created with an innate sense of smell that far exceeds, say, the ability to reason that skunks are not just creatively-striped cats wearing strange perfume.

Despite humans being accepted as the higher life form, we also know that forbidden fruit easily ends up looking better than the vegetable medley. Our obedience training becomes a life-long venture. Our free will and intelligence do give a great advantage, and being created in God's image and likeness especially elevates us. Yet we can sometimes follow our instincts too quickly and get spiritually skunked. Once we've learned that lesson, it only makes sense to say "Let us pray" before the skunks say "Let us Spray…" Dogs might not be able to store that lesson because scents and sense don't always connect.

How quickly I learned that you cannot reason with a dog. I wonder if God ever thinks the same about us in our weaker moments. He gave us reason, but we are also free to ignore its advice. Some pets serve as a form of security, and while Benny can announce the pizza delivery person with decibels that sound like a dozen opera stars doing vocal warm-ups in one phone booth, he's more of an announcer than a guard. A moment or two after the visitor's arrival, he quiets down and goes back to watching my every move. Watch dog, yes… he knows where I am in any given moment inside the house.

It occurs to me that sometimes we, as people of God, feel the need to defend our faith to non-believers or those who would prefer to persecute or mock what we profess. Like Benny on pizza night, I sometimes hear myself barking loudly and not saying much. That's when I know that I'm trying to do something myself instead of turning to the Lord for His grace. I might proudly brag that I'm trained to sit, stay, speak and even give you my paw at the Sign of Peace. But the command to love, the call to persevere in faith and not judge others is much harder to grasp, to teach and live. Jesus says "In the world you will have trouble, but I give you my peace." It's not **my** peace….but His gift. And it's important to sit and stay with that. "Good boy (or girl)… good sit….good stay….." Good God, do I appreciate that at times!

Fear has such a universal effect. When Ben was a puppy, he handled trips to veterinarian very well, licking the hand of the doctors and vet techs who gave him shots, even when they took his temperature in the most humiliating way. But as he grew, he came to be more skittish when lifted onto the cold metal table to be examined by the nice people in the white coats. (All my life my family mentioned that nice people in white coats might come for me. In my ignorance I just hoped they were referring to a visit by ice cream truck drivers, and quietly pondered what flavor of cone to order).

When my dog trembles, I have a hard time not feeling for him. I'm sure medical professionals who treat animals get used to it. What they also have to do—at least in front of the customer—is deal with our over-reactions. I cannot help but wonder if they have a lot of fun at veterinarian conventions telling "crazy pet owner" stories. I usually keep talking to Benny as the injection needle for booster shots comes near, but the more I do that, I discover that I'm really trying to calm myself more than my pooch. God seems to always be trying to free us from our fears. The voice of the master seems always so necessary, so welcome. Fear is useless, indeed; but it's so very common.

West Highland Terriers like Ben have large ears. They remind me of satellite dishes, and have a way of adding much to the expression of how he's feeling at a particular time. Sometimes, they're like sails that rest on the boat, but if I call his name, they perk up, springing to attention to catch my words. (How amazing and gratifying…and illusionary…to think that any creature would be so very attentive to one's words. Come to think of it, gosh, I just *love* having a dog)! When I have to put ointment in Ben's ears or some kind of cleaner, he can bend them backward and curl them. Like a two-year-old who sees a spoonful of cough syrup heading their way.

I'd like to think that I turn my ears *toward* God's voice every day, all day. But sometimes I'm more like a teenager hooked up to an iPod in the middle of a family dinner. Singers and songwriters either secretly wish or blatantly express a dream that people would be so attached to their music that it's their constant companion. It's too easy to know if a conscious person is responding to you. I sometimes, after anointing and praying for a person in a coma-like state will sing a verse of a hymn. They say we should presume that people retain the ability to hear to the end, and my prayer is often that the soul will be lifted up in song, even if there are no outward signs of a response. Seems to me that's how our loving Lord accepts our inner response to His communication with us.

The second Memorial Day after Benny joined the family, I had decided to drive out to the cemetery and visit my parents' graves. Having not read the posted signs as I drove in, I brought Benny to "meet" my parents. Mom always loved dogs, in contrast to Dad's pet peeves. As a girl, she had a mutt named Prince who, sadly, was hit by a car one day. Little Kass Murray ran to her pet in the street and quickly picked him up, but with his eyes closed in pain, he instinctively bit her hand, apparently reacting to his injury. But the moment he opened his eyes, he immediately released his grip, then died in her arms.

I was remembering that story as I trimmed the grass around my parents' grave stones and said a prayer. (And despite reports to the contrary, I did <u>not</u> make Benny kneel and join me...) Just before we were to get in the car, Benny suddenly lifted his leg and peed on my mother's grave. I was horrified, and though I couldn't blame his natural reaction to good, fresh grass, I soon saw the humor in it, as I could almost hear my mother laughing at the sight. And I could almost hear my father wryly saying "You know that's not what I meant by 'remember to water the grass'..." I could also hear Mom "That's okay, Benny---go for it"! Perhaps that day, St. Francis of Assisi took Dad for a walk in the gardens of Heaven to explain the dog-owner bond, and added, with a wink, the fact that dog is God spelled backwards.

Chapter Fifteen

SPEAK TO THE WORLD

One person whose treasury of writings I would love to see published in English is Blessed Fr. Michael Sopocko. This Polish priest was the Spiritual Director and confessor for St. Faustina. In her early mystical visions, Jesus showed her Fr. Sopocko before she had met him. Later, in her prayerful conversations with the Lord, he told her that Fr. Sopocko was indeed "a priest after my own heart." That inspired my song "Speak to the World":

Speak to the world about my Mercy
Every word a lifeline to the lost
Call them to my Tribunal where I forgive
Preach as you Trust me in my Mercy
That my grace bridges valley days across
As a priest after my own heart
They will not hear you, but their shepherd's voice!

While Blessed Michael, as a priest, could not divulge what they discussed under the sacred "seal of confession," his spiritual companionship with her had to be a profound blessing for him. At this point, my desire to read his books makes me either want to hire a Polish-speaking interpreter or start to study the language myself. It's quite striking that a number of saints whose spiritual directors/confidants/ co-workers in the Vineyard of the Lord end up canonized as well. When you think about it, our friends and family who progress in the ways of holiness can certainly assist in making us holier, if we let them! Think Francis of Assisi and Clare, Vincent de Paul, and Louise de Marillac. Sam the parish maintenance man and Isabel, the church secretary. Well, they're not *all* well-known, or canonized saints for that matter. But I hope you get the point!

I was privileged to attend the beatification of Blessed Michael Sopocko, priest. Having been to Poland once before, and being drawn continuously over the last decade deeper into devotion to Divine Mercy. Deciding to attend was an easy call. The trip itself provided some unforgettable moments. One of my favorite photos from the experience includes a candid shot of a large group of Polish nuns at a train station carrying two-liter bottles of Coca-Cola. We even convinced one of the sisters to pose as if she were chugging the whole thing. Dignified? No. Hilarious beyond language barriers? I think so. Shameless? Of course!

The journey to Poland was an East-West Catholic travel adventure. Fr. Bertha speaks enough Slavic languages to get us where we needed to be, which was very handy in the smaller towns outside of Poland's big cities of Warsaw and Krakow. Fr. Sopocko's beatification was held in Bialystok, so we had to travel by train across the Polish countryside. We were going to be changing hotels, so there was the burden of bringing our luggage on the train. At this point, the holy souvenirs were already challenging the strength of the suitcases. On our first trip to Poland, we bought so many sets of Mercy Chaplet beads (almost identical to rosaries) that the airport security mistook the chains for wires, apparently thinking it was a bomb. Fr. Bertha was paged to a special security office and made to open the suitcase himself. Luckily, the inspectors were familiar with prayer beads. I think they each went home with a pair, freshly-blessed.

About an hour before the outdoor Mass at Bialystok's Divine Mercy Shrine, which would be attended by 80,000 people, the priest concelebrants were gathered in the sanctuary to vest. A gigantic staging area had been built outside for this cool September day. After vesting, we had a significant amount of time before the procession would begin. As I looked to the right of the main altar, I discovered a lovely portrait of soon-to-be Blessed Michael on the wall. Walking closer, we found that his relics (his human remains/bones) were enshrined in a beautiful metal case in the wall.

"Hey—let's go pray over there," I said to Fr. Joseph. As providence would have it, the front pew, only about twelve feet from the relics, was not occupied at the moment. We settled in to pray and soon noticed that many of our brother priests had the same idea. The seating directly in front of Fr. Sopocko's relics was now quite full, and there were still about five hundred clergymen filing into the church. After praying for about ten minutes, I whispered to my friend that maybe we should move back and let some other priests have this close view. His response was what we jokingly call "New Yorker mode."

"I came half away around the world for this, and we got here first. I say we stay right here"! I couldn't argue with that logic, especially anticipating a lot of standing in the hours to come. Then, in what felt like just moment later, a group of men in business suits filed by the reliquary and lined up facing us. "Gee, Polish ushers are formal…" I thought…. "Why are they wearing sunglasses in church??" Just then, a suited gentleman walked in and knelt on a kneeler directly in front of Fr. Sopocko's bones. The slow-to-respond light bulb over my head went on: "Oh…they're secret service guys"! Fr. Bertha nudged me and whispered "Hey-that's the President of Poland"1

Instinctively, as I watched the security guards (not ushers after all) stand guard around him, I felt a sense of compassion rising within me for the burdens that leaders of nations must bear. At the same time, I was also inspired that this man who obviously was in attendance at this church ceremony as a political dignitary was right in front of us, deep in personal prayer. My years of doing Healing Masses and attending Charismatic conferences kicked in, and instinctively, my right hand was raised in his direction to pray over him. Surrounded by priests, in such a holy shrine, I just did this without much fore-thought.

Suddenly, a group of people standing on the left began photographing him as though he were an actor posing on the red carpet at the Academy Awards. Flashes of light and clicking shutters brought to my attention that the press had arrived. Then I realized that my hand was still raised, and I might end up on the front page of the Bialystok Beacon in this pose. Or, worse, find my gesture interpreted as some kind of threat to his security forces. Quickly, I lowered my hand, and my head, smiling at the strange scene that emerged from such a simple, prayerful moment. I admonished myself for ending my prayer so self-consciously, but was very grateful the next day when the Polish President's press coverage didn't include me at all!

On the train ride back to Warsaw after a glorious celebration of this holy priest and his elevation closer to official sainthood, we had another of those dramatic moments that I could have never imagined in my days as an aspiring screenwriter. As I said, Fr. Bertha and I had come in from another city (Krakow, and another Shrine of Divine Mercy) and were carrying our luggage on the train back to Warsaw from which we would fly home the next morning.

Though we had reserved seats and paid extra for a first class cabin (the only difference being not cushy seats but a promise of enough storage space for our bags) we soon realized that everyone else thought they made those same reservations. Coming home from a holy experience where God's Mercy, His greatest attribute is the central message, and dressed in our priestly garb, we figured it would be wrong to insist on our seats, and better to forgive the transportation company for over-booking.

We ended up sitting in the narrow hallway outside the first class cabins, balanced on top our suitcases, the kind of bags with four casters that make it easy to maneuver in airplane aisles and boarding areas. Everything was going well as we continued to marvel at the opportunity to be present for such an event. All of a sudden, the brakes of the train screeched as if we were slowing down to arrive at a station, but the sound then got increasingly louder and it became obvious that we were coming to a emergency stop. The pull of gravity sent us on our suitcase-seats careening down the train's hallway. The train came to an abrupt stop, going from a speed of about ninety miles an hour to standing still in about forty-five harrowing seconds.

After a moment's silence, passengers again began to chatter in a language I don't speak, so it was akin to being among people praying in tongues. But as five minutes turned to thirty, people's patience began growing thin. Someone slid a window open about half a foot, and we could see in the pitch-black countryside a railroad engineer with flashlights walking along the tracks and looking under the cars.

An announcement finally came, and I thanked God that one of us American priests could translate! It seemed that there was going to be a lengthy delay because the train hit something on the tracks. Then, we were given two choices; remain in the car for about two hours, or get off and walk to the next station where there was another train scheduled to depart in the direction of Warsaw in about fifteen minutes.

Just about everyone decided to get off and walk, which found people crowding toward the open door of the railroad car. But, arriving at the door, we found that, unlike a station stop where there is a raised platform, this situation led up to an open door and a need to jump down about four feet, in the dark, onto the piles of stone which made an uneven landing spot near the railroad ties. There's a certain panic that can set in during these kinds of emergencies, but I prayed that the number of priests and religious sisters present might keep everyone on their best behavior.

Arriving at the open door and the one step that normally leads to a platform; I saw that the jump was not a simple one. Then, to my relief I noticed that the people who reached the ground were then turning and assisting the ones behind them. After Fr. Bertha and I trustingly handed our luggage to merciful strangers, then leapt down onto the rocky surface, we turned to help those behind us. But what happened next reminded me of the phenomenon of a person who holds the door for others in places like Grand Central Station. A flow of people come through, and you start to wonder how to politely get a new volunteer to take his turn!

After one or two men and women were assisted by the two American priests, a huddle of Polish nuns started leaping into our arms like Sisters of the Divine Paratrooper! Of course, they didn't have parachutes, but one after another, these dear brides of Christ would see that we were priests and come flying at us like trained circus acrobats. Luckily, we didn't drop one nun! But I couldn't help but think: "Lord, these Polish sisters really take their 'Jesus I Trust in You' seriously....but if they knew how many gym classes were skipped in my life, they might not have trusted my strength so much!!"

When the train was empty, we found ourselves carrying our suitcases instead of rolling them, for there was no smooth surface to facilitate the use of the wheels. The night was very, very dark, and I have to say how I admired the ingenuity of those who whipped out their flip-phones to provide some light for the stumbling crowd.

At one point in this long, arduous hike Fr. Joseph said "O, Lord, Have Mercy"! I couldn't quite see him, and thought he had twisted an ankle, but he explained that he had just over-heard a conversation among the travelers concerning the real reason the train stopped—someone had jumped in front of the train. The delay was so that police detectives could come and gather evidence. We walked the rest of the way to the waiting train, mostly in silence, praying for God's mercy on that soul.

Try It, You'll Like It!

It's fairly universally accepted that there's nothing like a home-cooked meal. Restaurants have their place, but a girl in ruby slippers and gingham once spoke a truism that stuck---there's no place like home. I've heard husbands compliment their wives' culinary skills by saying that the meat loaf was just as good as his mother's. (I always watch her expression for a flinch…she may have tasted his mother's meat loaf and had to give an Academy Award-worthy performance to acquiesce to the home team….and humbly submit that the mother-in-law knows best! Even if said in-law was the type she secretly wanted to douse with a bucket of water…*just in case* she'd melt)!

My tastes in food are predictably Irish and, to some, terribly boring. My Dad was very happy with Mom's cooking, but consistently it was meat and potatoes, and one vegetable. Our ancestors had a long-held tradition of fairly bland food, and we consider a dash of salt and pepper quite an adventuresome addition for the taste buds. After all, what's life without taking risks from time to time? They say that variety is the spice of life, so then consistency is the *bland of life* on an Irish dinner plate. Still, there's no place like home! At our house, the conversation and laughter were the spice and salsa, though none of us knew what those flavors actually tasted like until we were young adults.

I've been blessed to travel further from the South Buffalo home base than most of my family. But my taste preferences have remained almost exactly the same. Squid? No thanks, I gave it up for Lent. Cayenne pepper? Wasn't she *Police Woman* in the 1970's?? Strange and exotic dishes don't tempt me at all. My dear friend Mr. Philos Park had an expression when faced with strange new food on his plate that has stayed with me: "It looks like 'Did I Eat It' or 'Am I Gonna….' "

After some coaxing and social pressure as a guest in someone's home, with an undercurrent of reminder that somewhere a child is hungry and would eat whatever is put before them, I have tried some new foods and was absolutely impressed. Other people's home cooking is great, and even in far-away lands, the courage to try can bring about a joy to the palette. Sometimes, I now find that I even forget to ask if they are serving potatoes!

That's-A Emm-A

Food in Italian-American restaurants can be wonderful, but in the chain stores it can be rather uniform and predictable. Before I ever needed or owned a passport, my first taste of authentic Italy was the day that I first tasted Emma Martelli's pasta. Home-made, hand-made, Heaven-sent! Emma was a sweet little lady, no more than four and half feet tall, but her skills with food were gargantuan. Her messages on my answering machine were sweet, always starting with "Father Bill---that's-a Emm-a". She first asked me to her house to visit her sick husband, Tony, and whenever I arrived, she would be cooking, regardless of the time of day. As soon as I finished praying, she'd have a plate of food in front of me, and say "Mangia! Eat"! The excuse that I had just eaten lunch ten minutes beforehand fell on deaf ears. She would watch me eat and ask "You like?" and in her broken English then add "Eat-a more—its-a delish!!!" When I visited Rome, and ate Italian food in its homeland for the first time, I instantly recognized Emma's authentic style of cooking. Mama Celeste and Chef Boyardee would run in shame to a near-by confessional after one forkful of Emma's food!

When I first met Emma Martelli, the mangia queen, her husband, Antonio (Tony) had already been ill when I first came to their parish, and I would bring him Holy Communion. One Sunday, she called me aside after Mass to tell me that Tony's doctor had recently indicated that his condition was quite serious, and his time with us could be short. She asked me to be the celebrant for his funeral when the time came. I was honored. Then, she wrinkled her nose and said "But don't use-a the 'cense…you make-a me sick"! It took a few seconds, but I realized that she was talking about incense. At first, I was perplexed, thinking that when I try to make sense, I was making her sick. Relieved, I made a mental note: no incense! Make sense, not sick a non-'cense funeral.

How Do You Spell Relief?

Once, in Slovakia, Fr. Bertha got us invited to dinner at the Byzantine cathedral in Presov with Bishop Jan Babiak. In advance of the trek, I had learned a simple musical refrain that is repeated throughout the Byzantine liturgy, and only one spoken phrase in the native tongue. The song was easy: "Alleluia, Alleluia…Alleluia, Alleluia". The phrase was a proverb that could be understood in Polish and Slovak. *"Svenia, Svenia, alla nasha svenia"* an earthly little proverb of the farming people that translates…. "It's a pig, it's a pig…. but it's _our_ pig"! Needless to say, the Bishop was much more impressed with my singing than the pig line. He gave Fr. Bertha a disapproving look and immediately suggested that he teach me a prayer in their tongue instead.

That night, the mother of the Bishop made homemade pierogies. His Excellency himself took our plates and served a very generous helping. These, to my Irish eyes, were pasta pockets with various, mysterious fillings. I gathered up the fifteen or so little treats and carefully cut them open. Rumor had it that sauerkraut was sometimes inside, and I had avoided that smelly shredded cabbage dish all of my life. Of course, as I cut into the third pierogi, I found a stringy, purple concoction rolling out onto my plate. I tried to pass it subtly to Fr. Joseph, but he whispered that it would be insulting to the Bishop and his mother if I didn't eat it.

"It's capusta!" he said… "Try it, you'll like it!"

Holding my breath, I tasted it. Expecting a foul taste, I was pleasantly surprised. How could something that stunk up the whole house when Mom made it for herself (she, and no one else including Dad ever ate it!) could actually taste good? After a while, I finished the last pierogi and set down my fork. Bishop Babiak then called out in Slovak and his housekeeper came from the kitchen, to my horror, with four more courses. Nobody told me that these were just the first course! In my house, pasta was an entrée, not an appetizer. I quickly found myself stuffed so full that I could have just spent an afternoon eating at Emma Martelli's house! I silently sang the chorus of my Christmas song *Make A Little Room* to my digestive system and forced myself to eat as much as I could. The proverb about the *svenia* was coming true in me!

The next night, we went for a wild ride through the countryside with the Bishop behind the wheel. The country back roads were rough, but his enthusiasm for acceleration didn't wane a bit. We stopped abruptly near a wooded area and he jumped out of the car with a plastic bag in hand to pick some fresh, wild mushrooms. They were huge-- so large that I half-expected a Cheshire Cat to appear and make the scene complete. I was secretly horrified that mushrooms would be on the dinner menu, because I could pretend to like sauerkraut, but all I knew about mushrooms was that my science teachers said they grow best on piles of manure. No thanks...but do Slovaks make gelato??

After a tour of several wooden churches of Slovakia, we pulled into a restaurant. Relieved that the mushrooms would stay in the car, we went in and were seated in a private room. After we ordered dinner, I realized that all the bottled water I had consumed along with the thrill ride in the Bishop's sedan meant that another short trip was in order. Quietly, I asked Fr. Joseph to find out where the rest room was. He asked the Bishop in the Slovak tongue, and there was some pointing and under-the-breath instruction. To my waiting bladder, it was a very long explanation. I wondered whether he had misinterpreted the question to be: "Tell me where your favorite fresh mushroom fields in the world are located". In the end, a simple translation came: "out this door, to the right".

I quickly excused myself and found a door right next to another that had the recognizable sign for a women's rest room. Trying the door next to it, I found it locked. So I took a walk around the restaurant, keeping an eye on the door. Several times, I tried the door, and it stayed locked. Ten minutes later, I was considering running outside to "water the mushrooms" because the door never opened. I hurried over and tried it one last time. Unable to speak the language at all, I couldn't communicate with the passing waiters and waitresses. Getting nervous, I hurried quickly back to the private dining room to find my English-to-Slovak interpreter. As I came in, the Bishop was regaling the room with a story. I prayed for a moment when I could politely interrupt.

Finally, the Bishop must have seen my expression of…uh…fullness. I told them that the men's bathroom was occupied, or locked, and he called over a waitress. She soon led me back out into the hall. On the verge of doing a jig to keep things from going from scary to humiliating, she led me *past* the locked door that I had been trying and then pulled back a blue curtain to reveal a door with the universally-recognized symbol for men's room. "Holy capusta!" I mumbled, as I ran in for bladder relief. Astounded that they would put a drape over the men's room door, I eventually calmed down and focused on gratitude.

While trying to sneak back into my chair at the table relatively un-noticed, the Bishop looked at me with an expression that seemed to ask "Success???" With no grasp of his language, I instinctively sang: "Alleluia! Alleluia! Alleluia! Alleluia"! It got a great laugh from the whole table, which of course, made me quite contented. Who ever thought a kid from Stevenson Street in South Buffalo would be doing schtick in the hinterlands of Slovakia??

Other Nations, New-Found Flavors

Landing in Ireland after an all-night flight was followed by the blessing of my first taste of Irish tea and scones, covered with Irish butter. It could have been the fact that plastic and rubber airline food was the only sustenance of the past several hours, but the tea was a delight, and the scone with raisins instantly became my new best friend. The taste of Irish butter made me want to buy a cow for the return flight! I've tried baking my own scones back in the states, but it's never quite the same. Even when a bit of butter makes the bitter batter better…

French cuisine gave me the most astonishing taste bud experience of my life. Of course, I was initially hesitant to try it. After some days on the road, my comfort food instinct for South Buffalo's Abbott Pizza and a cold Diet Pepsi was in full gear. Instead, a restaurant in Paris gave me a new taste of heaven. Fr. Joseph is fluent in French (though I did remember enough from high school language class to ask for the men's room…) and he had been in Paris several times.

I don't drink wine, but after some coaxing, agreed to have a glass. "You're in France," he kept saying, "believe me, you'll love it". I had heard this advice before and with best intentions, it wasn't always true. But I blame my narrow tasting guidelines, not my friends. We ordered steak, and a bottle of Bourdeaux. When the dinner came, Fr. Joseph instructed me to first take a bite of steak, then, before swallowing it, add a sip of the wine and see what happens.

Oooo la la!! I had ever tasted anything like that! For a moment, I had a vision of myself shoving packages of beef into my suitcases and bottles of French wine in every pocket of my coat before boarding the plane home. But reason won out---and baggage fees threatened to bankrupt me in that plan, so it sufficed to enjoy the meal in this far-away land, take my taste buds on a new journey, and count the blessing of this meal. Of course, chocolate mousse was the finisher. As Emma Martelli would say: "Delish!!"

No Raindrop Touched the Ground

⊱⊰⊱⊰⊱⊰⊱⊰

A window into Glory as the rain fell….
A vision of Our Lady in the night
the Virgin to the village let her silence tell
of consolation after famine's blight…

There she stood, interceding,
wrapped in prayer, not a sound
Still we come to be present, near the gable where
No Raindrop Touched the Ground,
near the gable where
No Raindrop Touched the Ground…

For many years the Irish eyes were crying…
for hunger stole our loved ones' very breath
St. Patrick brought the faith that transcends dying
For Hope in Resurrection after death…
There she stood….

She prayed before the Lamb upon an altar
a sweet reminder to the faithful flock
and now we pray with gratitude for those who
came celebrating Mass upon a rock…
There she stood….

Chapter Sixteen

NO RAINDROP TOUCHED THE GROUND

The Shrine of Our Lady of Knock in County Mayo, Ireland, is one of my favorite places in the world. My first visit there was very moving, and because I was with the tour group from Buffalo that included my sisters Eileen and Mary, it was extra-special to share that pilgrimage. Our parents never had the chance to visit the land of their ancestry, and until that week, none of my siblings or I had either. The priests on the trip took turns presiding at Mass, and I thank my lucky stars (or, as the cereal commercial says, "Lucky Charms"-they're magically delicious!) that it was my day when we went to Knock.

The story of the apparition recounts a dark, dreary, rainy night in August 1879 when some people from the village saw a vision on the gable (back wall) of the church. She did not speak, and sarcastic folks (like me, I confess!) later concluded that in a crowd of Irish townspeople, even the Mother of God cannot get a word in edgewise. But the real story is that sometimes when the Virgin Mary appears, the message is her prayerful, holy, motherly presence and yet she doesn't say a word. What's more consoling to human beings than their mother? And Ireland had been through the horror of the Potato Famine Blight with millions of lives lost. Millions had immigrated to other countries, and political upheaval was a constant as well; but the faith of the people remained firm.

I know that the Great Famine was one of the factors leading many Irish to embark on the journey to the US, so there was an awe that rose up in my heart to visit this shrine of healing and consolation. Patrick Quinlivan and Anne O'Gorman didn't meet and marry until they both came to America. And the apparition at Knock had not happened yet. One of my favorite elements of the story of the Virgin Mary's Irish appearance was that under the spot where she stood, after her departure, despite the rain, the ground was completely dry. The generous rains that make Ireland so green could be symbolic of countless tears shed as a result of the famine and/or "the troubles" of violent, terrorist bombings in Northern Ireland and beyond. The dry ground near the gable wall seems to remind us that our Holy Mother loves to console her children and dry their eyes.

My dear friend, Irish singing legend Dana Scallon and her husband Damien wrote what has become a favorite hymn for many, titled *"Lady of Knock."* I recorded it on my first CD and have loved singing it for many years. On one of my first visits to the shrine, Dana was in the congregation, and they asked her to sing her song after Holy Communion. As my God of surprises would have it, the regular organist was on vacation or ill, and the substitute musician was the one person in all of Ireland that didn't know *"Lady of Knock."* So Dana asked me to accompany her on my guitar.

Knock Shrine is gigantic, and even a great microphone can hardly make six strings sound like a fitting accompaniment, but the Lord blessed our musical collaboration. At one point, my left hand only half-pressed a string on the fret, and a nightmare of a buzzed note came through the speakers. I blushed my way through the final refrain, then quickly went to Dana to apologize. Gracious woman that she is, she simply said with a smile: "Father…it's always an honor to sing with you"! Believe, me the honor was and is all mine. But I accepted her compliment as proof that blarney spoken in a holy Irish place is transformed into a sweet blessing.

There's more to my first celebration of Holy Mass at Knock. I had just composed my first song on Irish soil, *Paintbrush in the Green*, and as I had the chance to preach, I also debuted the song at the Wednesday afternoon liturgy. Besides our tour group, there were about one thousand others in the basilica. Every Wednesday, the Sacrament of Anointing is offered. Apparently, bus-loads of Irish folk choose Wednesday for their pilgrimages for that very reason. So the place was filled with the demographic that would soon be the number-one audience for my music: elderly ladies!

Thankfully, the song came together very much as I had heard it in my head. I considered that the Blessed Virgin and a few angels did some post-production "sweetening" as the notes and lyrics floated out into the church. After Mass, scores of little Irish ladies came up to me with kind words about my song for Ireland. It was as if I had given them a gift, almost as if they had never heard a song about their country before. Of course, hundreds of songs had preceded my new tune with this familiar subject. Several even asked "Have you a recording of it, Father? Where can we get it"? not knowing that the ink was barely dry in my scribbled text with guitar chords.

Another aspect of that day that I recall with sweet joy is the part of the Mass where all the priests went out into the basilica to anoint the sick. The rector of the shrine made an announcement that when a priest came to each person, he/she should tell him their first name before he administered the sacrament. The people lined up quickly, and soon I could see that there were "people of all ages" as the first verse in "Lady of Knock" says in describing the original apparition;

families with young children and every other imaginable age.

As I began to anoint people, moving along a railing which separated the sanctuary with its rich green carpet from the pews, people spoke their names, with lovely brogues. Then, after about fifteen or twenty anointings, I noted a definite pattern that made me smile. "Pat.... Patrick... Patricia... Paddy... Pat... Patrick" Then, maybe one Bridget or Declan. And then immediately it came back to every variety of name based on Patrick that you could imagine. It tickled me so, and also spoke of the profound impact of that bishop-saint whom Americans honor too often with green beer and parades. The great legacy of St. Patrick, of course, is the faith that he taught. And I remind myself that his ministry has a direct connection to the fact that my ancestors were Catholic, and that I eventually became a priest.

An "Anointing" In Song

People sometimes refer to an "anointing of the Holy Spirit" when there's a special grace present in a gathering of believers praising the Lord. Like the holy fire of Pentecost, the Spirit of the Lord can descend and fill us in ways that leaves us in awe, in joy, and wonder, that will sometimes be applied to an unusually vibrant, clear, and challenging talk or homily. And sometimes, music and song can have an extraordinary impact or "anointing." Popular music and secular critics and audiences call it a "hit" or "favorite song." I believe that God can inspire us to create at times in ways that the writer/composer clearly feels the influence and guidance of the divine, and if we open ourselves to it, there's great grace to experience.

Dana has been inspired by the Lord to compose a number of really beautiful holy songs since her pop music career in the 1970's and the decades that followed eventually led her to use her musical gifts for God. I recommend her autobiography, *"Dana Rosemary Scallon: All Kinds of Everything"* (Copyright 2008, Gill & Macmillan, Dublin) for the whole story. Her openness to the Holy Spirit even led her to run for President of Ireland, and in her campaigns, she witnessed with Pentecostal Spirit and boldness for the dignity of human life in the womb, the sacred institution of marriage, and religious freedom.

One piece of music she wrote and recorded has a powerful anointing that sings out truth when you first hear it, and to me has God's fingerprints all over it. It's called "This Is My Body". She wrote it after hearing Fr. Frank Pavone of Priests for Life give one of those "anointed" talks at a pro-life conference where she was singing. He drew a connection between the words of pro-choice/pro-abortion activists that the decision of a mother to terminate her pregnancy and thus take the life of a child is her choice because "it's my body" to the words that Jesus spoke at the Last Supper: "This is my Body…"

Dana tells me that the song kind of flowed, even unfolding like a scene in her head as the lyrics were written and the melody played out. Its dramatic dialogue is expressed in three voices. One is the voice of a woman who had an abortion and later regretted it. The second voice is a pregnant mother defiantly announcing "No one can tell me what to do"! And the third voice is Jesus, the Merciful Lord who is the Truth. His "I give my life…a sacrifice of love for you" dramatically contrasts the one proclaiming a so-called right to choose who sings: "This is my life. I will not sacrifice my life for you…"

I've had the distinct privilege of singing the part of Jesus on several occasions. On Dana's recording, she sings it with California's wonderful Gretchen Harris and Mark Girardin a classically-trained tenor, taking the part of Christ. While at first, I saw a powerful symbolism of singing the part of Jesus as a priest, particularly the words that I pray each day in the Mass at the consecration of the Body and Blood of Christ. But when I attempted to sing along with the recorded track, I very quickly discovered that Mr. Girardin is a tenor, and I am ten or eleven steps lower in my most comfortable vocal range.

After several rehearsals, I stretched and warmed up my voice, but the higher notes were not within comfortable reach. But I didn't want to spoil the song, and it was too late to find someone else to learn it for that night.

When the instrumental backing track played during the concert at St. Amelia's church, I took a deep breath, said a prayer and opened my mouth. I could hear myself hitting the notes that I normally cannot perform, but as the song went on, I realized that it was like someone else's voice was coming out. This *might* indicate that Jesus is actually a tenor, but it was an experience in music ministry that I probably will never forget.

After the last note, in three-part harmony, the people in the church didn't just stand for an ovation, they jumped to their feet as though it were an act of praise for the Lord of Life. We rejoiced in the Spirit's anointing like the Apostles at Pentecost. Truly a God-moment.

In several performances of that song over the years, rehearsals were giving me pain in my throat, and Dana gave me permission to sing an alternate melody, wherever it was comfortable for me. A few years later, we did a concert for St. Luke's Mission's on my friend Wendy's 10th anniversary of death. Damien Scallon got the idea to have me stand behind the curtain on Villa Maria College's stage and not step through until the moment I began to sing my part, the words attributed to Jesus Christ.

Another idea, which added a new layer of symbolism and meaning was to have me fully vested as I would be for Mass. It was extremely effective, and again there was a special anointing. The combination of a special guest artist, an inspired song, the memorial for Wendy, a great number of the faithful, and the Holy Spirit all came together for another experience of song as prayer, as gift and joy, as anointing from above.

Towel and Pitcher and Bowl

❦ ❦ ❦ ❦ ❦ ❦

They had traveled dirt roads in the country
Carried sandals 'round fields in the grass
Sunk in sand by the Galilee seashore
Climbed the rocks at the Needle's Eye pass
Now the feet of those following Jesus
Will belong to Apostles soon sent
Taught to "shake the dust" when rejected
Learn to see what the Upper Room meant!

Watch the one who washes
Bending down to serve
Slave, but Love Incarnate
How this cleansing seemed absurd!
But His gesture's speaking example
It's a calling imprinting the soul
Do not miss the gift He's revealing—
It's more than Towel and Pitcher and Bowl
It's more than Towel and Pitcher and Bowl!

Chapter Seventeen

TOWEL AND PITCHER AND BOWL

Every year on Holy Thursday, there's a ritual in the Catholic liturgy where the presider washes people's feet. In Christ's time, the footwear and dusty streets on dry days and mud/clay mess of rain made it necessary and polite to wash your feet upon entering a home. In some circumstances, there were servants who washed the feet of guests. It was part of a warm welcome, and our modern American culture will probably not acquire this practice. The closest comparison would be modern homes with plush, white carpet where the hosts ask you to shed your shoes at the door. For some reason, I always panic—why didn't I call ahead to ask what color carpet they have??—and Murphy's Law means that my socks will always have holes in them. Sandals would solve that problem, but in Buffalo, New York that is only practical a few weeks each Summer. In winter, we'd need to medicate the frost-bitten feet of visitors, and that just seems like more than the most hospitable soul would care to attempt.

I wrote *Towel, Pitcher and Bowl* for a Holy Thursday homily while ministering at St. Gregory the Great. In my seminary years and first few Lents/Holy Weeks as a priest, there seemed to be rather heated arguments over who could or should have their feet washed. On one hand, traditionalists interpreted the gesture as referring to priesthood, since only men are ordained as Catholic priests, thus, only male persons should have their feet washed. Another interpretation says that all disciples are called to serve; so men, woman, and children should constitute the group of feet being washed. In addition, excruciatingly long liturgy committee meetings would discuss *ad nauseum* how many people could partake; twelve would point directly to apostles, priests, men-only. A number other than twelve would indicate the universal call to service and make the gesture more inclusive, less specific.

This lyric came from a moment in my personal prayer where I desired to look more closely at the gesture of Christ washing feet before reflecting on how best to respond to His words in that same Upper Room: "What I have done, You, too must do…" I've seen it done in several different ways, with a variety of effective simulations and symbolic expressions. And I also remember one of the priests at our seminary announcing, in rather dramatic style, that until he could wash women's feet, he refused to wash anyone's. To me, that seemed to politicize the religious meaning of the gesture. And it gave more attention to stirred-up dust of controversy than a focus on religious ritual on a day when we are meant to recall the holiness of Jesus' washing the Apostles/disciples feet. It almost made me want to wash my hands of the whole foot-washing concept. But then, remembering Pontius Pilate washing his hands, I decided to write a song and try to re-direct our attention back to what Jesus did.

At the International Priests Retreat in Ars in 2009, they incorporated a foot-washing ceremony into the day when we also renewed our priestly promises. There was a profound talk that morning by Jean Vanier, the founder of L'Arche, a community of believers whose loving service is to the physically, mentally, and emotionally-challenged. Vanier had over 1,500 priests, bishops and cardinals rapt in wonder as he told stories of how serving the people our world sees as deformed and useless has taught those who minister to them to see Christ in their faces. It taught us to realize that our own weaknesses and flaws might not be as visible or tangible, but they're just as real!

After the talk, we prepared for a procession to a large, open field outside the gigantic hall. We were carefully instructed that we were to do so in complete silence. Thousands of chairs were set up in small circular groupings of about twelve seats, and we were quietly and prayerfully to walk to those places. After all were in place, a supply of towels, a pitcher of water and a basin in each section were to be taken by one priest who would first remove his outer vestments. He would then silently wash the feet of a brother priest, and afterward, the priest who was washed would stand and lay hands on the priest who washed him. The sun was shining brightly on this inspiring ritual, as we prayerfully followed the instructions and interceded for one another.

While I sat and waited my turn to have my feet washed, I tried to be fully present to the moment. I smiled, thinking that it was no small miracle that all these clergymen who had been enjoying much conversation all week could now observe such wide-spread silence. The sun was particularly hot that day and my Irish skin was telling me that its ability to broil (I can burn in the time white bread needs to be toasted....) was near. I asked the Lord to do something about that, and then, looking up, saw a very small cloud gently gliding across the sky over us. I watched it for about twenty seconds as it headed right to the spot where it would block the direct sunlight. It seemed to linger there just long enough for me to know that somebody heard my prayer. Wow! He is good!

The outdoor foot-washing at Ars remains for me a very vivid memory every Holy Thursday. For priests to minister to each other is a humbling opportunity. Christ recognized that our need to be served by another is as vital as our attempts to do so for our people. There's a very practical reason why priests cannot give themselves sacramental anointing or absolution in confession. There's a powerful perspective in our humanity as well as an essential element to Christianity to not be self-serving. It takes an effort to ask a brother priest to do that for you. And it's completely humbling to be asked.

In the field at Ars, the next day, we had a communal penance service. Before they announced this, I had hoped earlier in the week to receive the mercy sacrament inside the little church where St. John Vianney spent endless hours ministering to repentant sinners. This priest practically lived in his confessional, and people waited hours in line to have him hear their confessions. Admittedly, it was a romanticized notion to desire to go to confession in Vianney's actual confessional. I heard them announce early in the retreat that there would be priests in the confessionals inside the church throughout the day, but every time I stopped in, the confessor's seat was empty. They must have been on a break for fresh crepes or chocolate mousse.

After finding the confessionals un-occupied four or five times, I resigned myself to the *Little Confessional on the Prairie* experience. (Being an American raised on 1970s TV, when they referred to it as the prairie, my mind for one-liners already started flowing: "Bless me Father, for I have sinned. I pushed Nellie Olson in the mud but she *deserved* it...") After praying for a while, I joined the line of priests near the outdoor confession benches, duly noting the gift of a cloudy sky compared to the glaring brightness of foot-washing day. The Lord always has me covered--and this day I praised his creation of clouds that kept us from sunburn while simultaneously holding back raindrops.

When my turn came, I approached a priest who was sitting on a bench; he was vested with a traditional purple stole. When I began to speak, I suddenly realized that he didn't know English. And while, to some of the faithful this could be considered an easy way to go to confession, I kept walking and asked another, then another. Actually, it was about eight or ten. They were Korean, Spanish, Vietnamese, French, and almost every other imaginable nationality. Ever more aware of the Church's cultural diversity, I was getting frustrated and more than a little embarrassed.

Finally, I overheard another priest (who looked younger than I) saying to several purple-stoled ordained multi-nationals "Do *you* speak English"? We almost literally bumped into each other in the center of the field, feeling like Charlie Brown after Lucy has pulled away the football a dozen times. I answered him: "None of these priests speak English"! "Yes, he said…I know. I'm looking for the same thing…" We stood there for a moment, and then I recognized the obvious answer to both our prayers. So we found a quiet area of the field and offered each other this beautiful sacrament. God speaks every language, but my skills are limited to just one. I was grateful that he had me covered again.

Ministry as service is, as the *Towel, Pitcher and Bowl* lyric says, more than towel and pitcher and bowl. It's more than chasuble, alb, and stole, too. Being a servant of the gospel calls us sometimes to unusual places and situations, surprises and challenges. We serve men, women and children. And together, we all serve our God. Sometimes, like the original Apostles, we have to shake the dust from our feet when the message and messenger are rejected. At other times, we need to persevere in faith, for we may find that the answer to our problem is standing right next to us. It's more than towel, pitcher, and bowl. But a great tradition began with those simple household implements of welcome and cleansing.

Listen

৵৵৵৵৵৵৵

Listen in the waiting, watch the night grow dark
Believers become beacons, to spread the Spirit's spark
All our Advent songings, cry for Christ's pure light
Our deepest well of longings, bemoan un-focused sight

Listen in the Winter, put plans to hibernate
Receive bouquets of quiet, let rest regenerate
Seek joy in contemplation, like bundled kids love snow
Sip time alone with Jesus, watch grace in your life grow.

Chapter Eighteen

LONGINGS AND SONGINGS

We who make music and love God could really do an in-depth retreat and study of what type of songs speak to our souls at any given moment. It's one of the reasons that songwriters keep writing and singers keep creating tunes. Sometimes a song you've composed seems as if it could be just for the writer, him or herself. The expression of personal emotions seem too fragile and vulnerable to risk sharing with others. Yet, in many other situations, a lyric or a melody will reach someone in a deep, personal place. And it's hard to predict which song will do that. It's very different from person to person, listener to listener.

Whether I buy a new collection of music by a favorite artist or give someone unknown a try, there's an inner gauge of measurement that automatically activates in me. Sometimes, from the first line of a lyric, I'm totally drawn in, relating personally to what is being sung. At other times, I am taken by surprise by the blunt honesty of a phrase, or in the case of many of my favorite singers/writers, I'm amused, pleasantly surprised and delighted in the heart. In the mysterious process of making music, I often feel rather clueless about how it will end up. Then, in certain moments, I sense that it's only partially my decision where a song heads. I feel more like a companion in that creative moment than an author.

Amy Grant has been quoted in interviews that sometimes, while singing her own songs, she has to almost emotionally detach from what she's doing so as not to become overwhelmed and unable to sing. In order for an audience to get their chance to respond, they have to hear it. I can relate to that inner struggle when singing. Though Amy and I were born only weeks apart (birthday class of 1960) I would never compare my own work to hers. (But then, they do say that imitation is the highest form of flattery...so I *want* to write great songs like Amy's that touch hearts, since her music has so often moved me profoundly).

I chose to sing Amy's song *I Don't Know Why* during the funeral for my nephew Jimmy who died at age 13 in a tragic all-terrain vehicle accident. Undoubtedly, the single saddest event in our family's life was the loss of this vibrant young man who had just entered his teens about three weeks earlier. In my prayer and preparation, a friend forwarded an e-mail with a quote from St. Pio of Pietrelcina (popularly known as "Padre Pio") that truly helped anchor my fears and grief for the task of presiding and preaching.

Padre Pio said that in the face of life's greatest tragic heart-breaks, our natural response is to ask "why," but we may never find a satisfactory answer to that question while on earth. He said that it is better for us to ask ourselves "What are we to do now?" While the overwhelming torrents of sorrow might not bring any kind of answer for a long time, as life trudges on we see that our life's ongoing search for purpose, meaning , love and comfort are not over until we go home to God. The "now" moment is our time of decision, and the land of "why" can be a prison.

I'll admit that I sometimes *have* to lean on music as a device to help get me through the most difficult celebrations of funerals. For some reason, if I break a song into parts, sing a verse or refrain, then speak/preach, I can get through it a bit more easily. Singing forces us to concentrate on controlling our breathing, and, for me, it raises my focus to something beyond myself, and helps keep me from blubbering incoherently. I know that we cannot always control our emotions, and have great empathy for people who get up to do eulogies and I have a hard time getting a sentence completed without sobbing. It makes me wish that I had offered them the advice to sing a little in between each part.

Listen in the forest, footsteps in the wild
Alone in nature's splendor, be simple, as a child
Foot prints in snow carpet, heavenly scent of pine
A doe observes your yearning
For streams of Love Divine...

Will the Lord speak?
Will you let Him,
His abiding grace will suffice
All too often, we live like we forget
That God is with us, Jesus Christ!

I don't know why life can be such a place of frightful emotional roller-coasters. But I *do* know that music does sooth me when I need it. One time, a lady told me that she enjoys my CDs because they help her relax and get to sleep. Now, I have to say that her comment makes me wary of singing during Sunday homilies. For while just a wee bit of snoozing in the pews for insomniacs can be a gift, we wouldn't want to promote that as a norm! But I can accept that it was not an adverse reaction to my songs that may lull people to a peaceful, relaxed state. If sleep follows, it must mean it's needed.

Mom always loved the music of my Irish friend, Dana. At one point in her confinement to the skilled nursing facility, she was experiencing a rough patch of attempts at pain management. She was unable to eat or drink, and unconscious for most of the day. She was actually admitted to Hospice care, but, ironically, would be discharged from their care a month later for not dying; she "graduated" from end-of-life care and she lived five more years, actually!

One afternoon while I was sitting at her bedside as she slept, she slowly opened her eyes, took my hand and said softly "Sing **Lady of Knock**!" A song request, out of the blue! And there I was, asked to sing for the woman who used to have her children sing for the nuns when they visited, whose own voice sang us to sleep in our cradles. Foremost in my mind was that she might have been fading from this life at any moment. When your parent is in that situation, your instinct is to do whatever they ask, especially if it could make her a bit more comfortable. I took a few deep breaths, and sang it through, as she drifted back to sleep. We often speak of "comfort food," but I firmly believe that there are also "comfort songs", a musical feast for the spirit.

Several years later, July 7th, 2008, the day Mom did go home to God, we had a CD of Dana's songs playing softly, and I kept hitting the "start" button as the afternoon went on. About six months after Mom's passing, I had an opportunity to visit Dana and Damien Scallon (her husband, co-author of the song) and shared that I had sung it not only at her bedside and played the CD throughout her final day, and that we also included it in her funeral liturgy and the congregation sang it in a beautiful chorus. Later that year, the mother of one of my brother Joe's best friends died. At the wake, her daughter told me that they were playing one of *my* CDs as her mother prepared to leave us for the greenest of pastures. (Heaven, not Ireland. She was about to travel to the place where one takes no baggage...) I now know what the expression "You could have knocked me over with a feather" means. But you could also ask me to sing "Lady of Knock" and I'd always be tickled.

A Private Audience

My pastor at St. Teresa's at the time of my ordination was Father Ted Berg. He was a skilled parish administrator, a very good preacher, and a whole lot of fun to be around. For years, he teased me mercilessly about my collection of church lady friends from daily Mass. ("Do you have *any* friends in this parish without grey hair"?) In turn, I would feign an apology that he had to deal with their bereft state after the proverbial announcement upon my departure, akin to "Elvis has left the building!" But his quick come-back was always a promise to try to keep their spirits up until I could return.

When Fr. Berg was diagnosed with cancer, countless people prayed for him. He decided to retire a bit early in order to combat the disease, and for several years he endured treatments with great grace and dignity and his unique brand of humor. Unfortunately, word came that the medical professionals could no longer offer hope of treatments to keep the cancer under control. He moved to a beach house that he owned on Lake Erie in Hamburg, NY essentially to prepare for his death.

One morning while praying for him, I felt an urge to go and visit Fr. Ted that day. As soon as that thought came, another immediately followed: bring your guitar and sing him one of your songs about priesthood. I had heard from some priest friends that these songs seemed to offer them encouragement and affirmation in their vocations. While Ted and I were friends for years, I didn't even know if he had ever heard any of my music. When we got together for lunch or I was back at the home parish for a visit, I had never sung for him. And it seemed quite awkward and embarrassing (and more than presumptuous) to just walk into his home with my guitar.

I put my guitar in the trunk, and decided to get a feel for the situation before bringing it inside. We chatted for about forty-five minutes, laughing most of the time and kidding just like old times. But I chickened out, convincing myself that he hadn't *asked me* to sing to him. I chastised myself for what was apparently another case of my out-of-control musician's ego craving attention or a pat on the back. At the end of our visit, I asked him for his blessing, and he asked for mine. I sensed that this might not be our last visit, for he was still able to get around, though appearing weaker after months of cancer treatment. He insisted on walking me to the door to prove that he was still in the game as it were.

A few weeks later, on my day off, I called my friend Cheryl McNerney who had become Fr. Berg's care-giver and actually moved into his house to be with him in his need. She told me that he was continuing to decline, and I had her ask him if he was up for a visit. She came back to the phone and said yes, then added that his strength was pretty low, so she suggested I keep it brief. As I gathered what I might need for various errands on my day off, the idea to bring the guitar hit me again, quite a bit stronger than the first time. And I knew in my heart that I didn't listen to the Lord's prompting the first time.

The prophet Samuel had to hear the Lord's call several times until it dawned on him that it was God calling, not Eli the temple priest. As this story came to mind, I decided that I really had to surrender to the call this time. All the way there, I was conversing with myself (or was it my conscience??) that I would keep the guitar in the trunk of the car, and then ask if he'd like me to sing him a song. If he said yes, I would go out and get it. If he didn't feel up to it, I would just change the subject and probably not feel as foolish as I would if I had to lug a guitar case in and out without needing to use it.

As I parked my car, the clouds of confusion and self-doubt cleared and, in a moment of clarity, I decided to be obedient and just bring my instrument in. If Fr. Berg declined the offer of a song, I would at least be satisfying the Lord's nudging, as His voice in my heart that at this point was almost nagging me. So, after exchanging pleasantries, I strapped on my guitar, as I told him that I felt like the Lord was asking me to sing for him. He was completely open to it. I chose *Another Christ* because it attempts to connect the priestly call back to Christ and the Apostles at the first Eucharist, and then offers a narrative/synopsis of a priest's life and ministry from discernment of the initial vocation call through to his death.

ANOTHER CHRIST
Upper room at night, the Lord and Master said
"when you drink this cup, when you eat this bread…
Do this…follow me, that they may be fed.
I'll send you as my witnesses when I'm risen from the dead.
First He called each one by name, to much more than they deserved
And He promised to remain, as He gave the gifts to serve…
With an undivided heart, come to see His grace suffice
Jesus consecrates each priest, for to be another Christ…

Young man's room at night, Holy Spirit sings
You'll contradict the world, come set aside all things
The Lord has plans for you, vocation's heart-phone rings
Your leap begins with "yes," so hold on to Gabriel's wing!
For He calls each one by name…

Rectory room at night, wrestling with despair
Feeling so inadequate for people's sins to bear

The walk in faith precarious, with knees worn out in prayer
Yet Christ rejoices in your heart, it's His shepherd staff you bear!
Since He called each one by name...

Hospital room at night, breath and pulse decreased
Angels and saints around, Heaven prepares the feast
His mind plays the scenes of life, graces that never ceased
Souls that he touched converge to welcome a holy priest!
For He called each one by name...

When I finished singing, there was a rather long silence. Then, my friend Fr. Ted said "Sing it again, Bill". He told me that the line "hold on to Gabriel's wing" really touched him, and so I sang it again. From the first notes, I sensed a flow of the Holy Spirit in the song, as well as the deep, abiding peace that comes when our soul knows that we are doing what God calls us to do, a recognition of His will. How difficult it can be to trust that instinct, but the blessings that come when we do are a terrific reminder that He uses us, if we cooperate with His grace, if we hold on to Gabriel's wing!

As I started driving home, I was praising God for His persistence. And very grateful to have had the privilege of ministering to a man who had served me and so many others. I also had a strong sense that this would be my last visit with Fr. Berg, and it was. Years later, I continue to be awed by his response to that song. It was like a very young child having someone read a story book, where you finish, begin to close the book and the child speaks one of the few words they know: "Again"! In the experiences where we see that, we have heard the voice of God and followed it. Can we not almost hear him saying: "Again—keep listening, keep following"!

Chapter Nineteen

THERE'S A HOME

In the last week that Mom was conscious, she kept saying that she wanted to go home. And, of course, being sometimes very literal people we said: "Mom, we *sold* the house four years ago. This is your home". She'd just look at us and say "Oh…" and a moment later would add: "I want to go home!" She had been living in a skilled nursing facility for almost seven years, and from the first day of admission never once asked us take her out of there, or, specifically, to return home. In fact, she made the very best of a difficult and painful situation of separation from the house where she lived for over forty years.

We realized eventually that in what would be her last few days that she wasn't talking about 205 Stevenson Street. She was talking about the home that we all want to go to someday. In the prophet Isaiah we hear "The Lord of hosts will provide for all peoples….God will destroy death forever". In a Gospel passage I've preached on hundreds of times, Jesus says "In my Father's house there are many rooms…I'm going to prepare a place for you". The Lord had always provided a home for Kass Quinlivan, though during the

185

Great Depression her parents had to keep moving because they could not afford the rent. The size, shape, and number of rooms in whatever home we live, the people we share it with, if we're blessed (as the Quinlivan family was) to stay in one place for many years, reminds us that these homes and the love we experience in them are a foretaste of the home that's prepared for us in eternity. There, the rent is paid forever, and the landlord is the Lord of the Land!!

I was praying in my chapel at the rectory on July 1st (six days before my mother's death) and said "Lord, do you want me to write a song in case something happens to Mom"? …and her recent request for homecoming immediately surfaced. So I wrote:

There's a home, a place of perfect peace
For our souls, O land of life's increase
For those longing just to see God's face
Fed on earth by each taste of Grace
Where there's no more weeping, no losing…only keeping
Meek, the kings and peasants
Made holy in God's presence….Home… Sweet… Home!

A few of us had the blessing and privilege of being with Mom as the Lord took her home. As she breathed her last, very peaceful breath, my sister Mary said it was like a veil was lifted; the color of her face changed. That's why for her funeral Mass we chose a reading from the prophet Isaiah that speaks of the promise that the Lord will lift the veil for all those who believe: "On that day, behold (we will say) our God to whom we looked to save us.."

The lyric from the refrain of the song that I prayed with all week before her funeral says: "O land of life's increase". We always pray for life….my mother was a great respecter of life. She lived her life with gusto, and she knew that it was a gift from God. I sensed that she would have wanted us, on the day of her burial to be truly praying with gusto, praising God for Her life, for our own and how they're connected, and for all the lives we have shared. She also would have wanted us to sing really loud during the liturgy. Mom loved to sing and was at home in a good song!

At my brother Pat's wedding in 1981, Mom's brother, my Uncle Jack Murray, who, like me, did not need to be asked twice to get up and sing a song, did just that after the sound system had finished playing. He climbed up on a chair, to be heard by the crowd. Uncle Jack had a partial hearing loss, which made him speak and sing with greater volume that most. Kass, as the younger sister not to be outdone, did him one better and stood up on a table! My brother's in-laws had not seen the Murrays at a party. Because it was a formal affair, neither Mom nor Uncle Jack swung from the chandeliers. But if one did, the other would have tried to top that!

Kass Murray Quinlivan was also never afraid to give a witness to her friends, figuratively to stand up to proclaim and sing out what she believed. I remember as a child, walking through the kitchen when she was on the phone and hearing her say: "You *have to* forgive if you're a Christian!" Mom preached the Good News of Christ, long before I did…because she believed it long before I existed, and kept deepening that faith for 85 years. She believed all her life; and she had great love for our Lord and the Church. I remember thinking while Fr. Dan (Young, her "other priest son") was proclaiming the Gospel at her funeral Mass, that after I was ordained, one day I asked Mom if she wanted me to come and say a Mass at the house. She said "No—I heard that it's not allowed!"

I answered "But you're not well enough to leave home. I think I can do this". She said: "Just bring me Holy Communion. I don't want you breaking the rules and getting in trouble"! Months later, I did finally talk her into a home

Mass, and my friends from St. Luke's came and did the music. And she loved it. And she said "OK—you can do this again"! For much of her adult life, and especially once her children were raised, Mom attended daily Mass. In her later years, and during my periodic unemployed and between-job periods, I often accompanied her.

The day my 5 siblings and me met to make final decisions on the details of Mom's funeral, we debated whether to go to the funeral home that morning or not. My sister Eileen spoke a word that sounded like Mom's wisdom reminding us of what she had taught all our lives: "The Mass is the most important part"! If we could teach that to the next generation of believers, there wouldn't be a need for any more church closings or mergers.

While we live as mortgage-holders
We owe, we owe, so off to work we go...
Learning love, we are God's own soldiers
Our room's prepared and the Lord can't wait to show..
There's a Home........
Where there's no more sorrow, No "wait until tomorrow"...
No more pain of losses
So pilgrims, bring your crosses...
Home.... Sweet.... Home!

My mother's 85 years of life were full, mostly, full of love. What amazed my family and me during the seven years of convalescence was that she was still making friends and adding to her collection of relationships. In the skilled nursing facility, she'd introduce the woman from housekeeping as "my friend, Betty". I recall how they seemed touched: "Kass, am I really your friend"? "Of course," she'd respond, "you empty my garbage can, you come to visit me every day and I appreciate all of that"!

Mom's life was full of music. She didn't play an instrument but she loved to sing. Aunt Edna, her dear sister, played the comb. A little-known art form, it consisted of wrapping a piece of toilet tissue around it like a kazoo. The Depression-era "greatest generation" lived life so simply, and wanted their children to have a better life. Most of them did; my cousin Joe is an accomplished kazoo player, and as the son of a comb-player, that's a step up! None of Kass and Jim's kids made music with hairstyling implements. Though in the 1970's our blow-dryers could have been interpreted as bathroom mirror virtuoso performances as the lyrics of our favorite pop tunes were sung and the brush became a microphone.

In the era of transistor radios and record players, before Mom discovered the joy of having us spare her ears by using headphones, she'd often pick up the melody of the songs that we heard on the radio. But like other members of the Swing generation, she complained that she couldn't understand the lyrics of rock and roll "bang-bang, crash-crash music" as she dubbed it. So Paul McCartney and Wings' song *"Band on the Run"* became *"Stand on the Rug."* We laughed ourselves silly at her interpretations, or should I say, sillier? Once a wrong lyric came out, it was hard to re-learn. Even the refrain of the Frankie Valli classic *"Can't Keep My Eyes Off of You"* that goes 'I love you baby...' became "I love you MADLY" in Mom's version.

When she wasn't singing, she was humming. Quite often, the humming came so naturally to her that she'd be humming and not even be conscious of it. Standing in line at a wake, sitting at a PTA meeting, Mom would hum. Her daughters, as I recall, in that teenage phase where everything your mother does is SO embarrassing and un-cool, used to say to her: "Mom! You're HUMMING"! She'd smile, stop for a moment, and then it would begin again. "What's wrong—you don't like *'Stand on the Rug'*"?

We had a lot of fun in our house, and a lot of faith, too. Our home version of religious devotions were just normal in our family. It wasn't until we were older that we found out many families didn't hold May Crownings in their living room as well as attend the ceremonies at church. I presumed that every Catholic household had statues on the mantle, St. Joseph on the right and Blessed Mother on the left of the fireplace, just as in church! We always had the nuns for dinner. I'd say to my friends "Last night we had nuns for supper …they were delicious"! My Aunt, Sr. Mary Kathleen, used to come home from Rochester to visit and in those days the sisters didn't travel alone. That was back in the peak era of The *Sound of Music*. Mom would have the 6 of us get up and sing for the sisters. I have vivid memories of that… and can still do the whole "So Long, Farewell" routine, including "cuck-oo…cuck-oo.."

Having always loved *The Sound of Music*, my only fear was that Mom was some day going to take the curtains and make play clothes for us…and then make us wear them when the nuns were coming! After Sister Kathleen died, we'd have the Mercy sisters from St. Teresa's, Sr. Elenore Kam and Sr. Virginia Marie Grasso. The sisters were great company, and there was always a lot of laughter when they visited. And dessert! In Mom's nursing home years, Sr. Virginia Marie repaid the favor, bringing delicious meals several times a week so Mom wouldn't have to pretend to eat the institutional food.

My mother always had a tender place in her heart for the needy and down-on-their luck. We had a little statue of a friar on the mantle (much smaller than St. Joseph and the Virgin Mary…) with a string tied around his finger and a message painted on the base: "Give to the Poor". Mom was very generous to people on the street who asked her for money; she loved them like Jesus does…without asking questions. She knew what it was like to be hungry or have little food in the house. Her family lived in poverty during the Great Depression, and she reminded us always how blessed (spoiled!) we were. She'd be just as giving when a down-on-their-luck person was honest in asking for a dollar and admitted that they were going to have a beer with it. "Okay-- have one on me," she'd say.

Whenever her grandchildren or nieces and nephews came to our house, she'd try to slip them a dollar when my father wasn't looking—even though he knew what she was doing. When my cousin Rocky Molloy and his wife Linda's kids saw her in a store, they reported to their parents: "We saw our *dollar aunt.*" Mom was always adept at reaching out to people who she thought were in need, sometimes before they even asked for assistance. One of our favorite stories comes from Buffalo's infamous Blizzard of 1977. Looking out our front picture window, she noticed two people struggling against the fierce, bitter, snowy wind, attempting to cross the sidewalk in front of our house. The poor souls kept stopping while turning their backs to the wind. Heads covered in scarves, they were obviously losing strength in the fight, so Mom got their attention and waved them in.

It was two young mothers, hoping to get to the store for milk for their babies. Mom jumped into action, offering them dry clothes, tossing their clothing in the dryer, making tea and offering them most of the milk that we had. She was suddenly like a Christian with a new-found mission---save the blizzard victims! About ten minutes later, a little lady was doing the same thing out front, so Mom called her in, and prepared to warm and serve her. It all felt so rewarding until the woman removed her hat and scarf and we recognized that it was Fran Schultz, the lady who lived next door. "Ohhhh!" she gasped "I was *almost home*. What do you *need*, Kass"? Oooops. Even fired-up missionaries make mistakes!

While we claim our own earth-bounded addresses
We sleep secure, relaxed in favorite chairs
We'll be more at home where God's hand caresses
To Him we'll fly on wings of answered prayers

Mom lived a life that took chances. In fact, she probably took chances on every church's raffle in the diocese of Buffalo and surrounding area! But she taught us to take chances: "Go ahead… try it. You can do that"! I hope that all of you have had someone in your life who encouraged you the same way. Perhaps it was the experience of living through tough times that made my mother adventurous. Or it could just be that she was born with a love for fun. When she was a child and got into trouble in St. Monica School (undoubtedly, for talking…) the nun punished her by making her sit under the teacher's desk. Five minutes later, the Sister stood and walked to the chalkboard and fell on her face. Guess who tied her shoes together???

When Kass was dating Jim Quinlivan, and they were getting close to engagement, one of her friends asked her "Does Jim have a temper"? and she set her mind to finding out. They were going to a party at a cottage at Crystal Beach. Dad came down the stairs dressed in a neatly-ironed white shirt. Mom pulled a ripe tomato from behind her back and threw it at him, which exploded on impact. So much for the nice white shirt! With an annoyed look and groan, he simply turned around and went back upstairs to change. He came down several minutes later and she asked "Are you gonna forgive me"? "Yes," Dad said, "but please don't do that again". So Mom took a chance with Dad, and he obviously took one, too, getting married May 2, 1953, in St. Teresa's church.

On a more serious note, I want to share something very beautiful that my mother experienced a few months after Dad died. She had been diagnosed with bladder cancer. After the surgery, she experienced several days of mystical experiences in her hospital room. It began one day in Mercy Hospital's intensive care unit when she awoke and asked us if Trocaire College (which is next door to the hospital) was having a concert. "I can hear the choir," she said "but they must be rehearsing. They keep singing the *Battle Hymn of the Republic*. It's beautiful, can't you hear it"? We didn't, but she did. Constantly!

After eight days, hearing it day and night, she prayed "Lord, enough of that one. Don't your angels know any other hymns"? After a moment, the music did change, to a medley of songs that she knew from her childhood, even including, incredibly, *Take Me Out To The Ballgame*. Her experiences included visions of the head of Christ crowned with thorns, images of soldiers covered in dust, a wall of bricks with the names of her loved ones who had pre-deceased her, and a screeching serpent. After the more frightening and disturbing elements, the Lord would "change the channel" as Mom said, and show her beautiful scenes of a neighborhood with homes decorated with Christmas lights.

It all started with the *Battle Hymn of the Republic*, as Mom's final few years entered a new kind of battle. We closed her funeral Mass with the obvious choice of the *Battle Hymn* as our recessional, and I asked that everyone present sing it with gusto, as Mom would have sung it for the Lord's glory. I even suggested that some may want to stand up on the kneelers or pews, in her memory. But I asked that they not get up on the table. This was not Pat's wedding reception.

Mom was "baptized in the Holy Spirit" years ago and received the gift of tongues. Not everyone in her life knew that. She didn't talk about it much. But during her years in Mercy's Skilled Nursing unit, her room was a few floors above the Emergency Room. And she would tell me that sometimes in the night, she would awaken, praying in tongues rather loudly, like a battle cry. It's what we sometimes call "prayer warrior tongues". She'd be concerned the morning after because she had no idea what she was saying, but figured that if this was the Lord's idea, and if he was using her prayer, it was okay with her. She was mostly concerned that it didn't wake up all the other residents!

Whenever she would experience this, it seemed that one of the nurses would later share that Mrs. So-and-So down the hall was struggling all night and had died. A few times I would arrive and recall a news story from the night before (an accident, fire, or near-drowning) where the person was taken by ambulance to the E.R. a few floors beneath her room. It seemed that God was teaching Mom that He could creatively use her through prayer, even when she was confined to a bed and unable to walk. I'm a firm believer, and Mom was, too, that we should not waste our suffering but offer it to the Lord with Christ's passion and cross for His higher purpose and will.

In the years after I became a priest, Mom would occasionally instruct me on what *not* to say at her funeral Mass. I hope she's forgiven me for just one not-so-veiled reference to a certain hobby. In the time that I was given to preach and reflect on her life, I'd only been able to "scratch-off" the surface... And I believe that the Lord Jesus is surely giving her a WIN, taking her to a PLACE, and SHOW-ing her the results of her life's photo finish. She loved all His creatures but especially horses. And she mostly enjoyed how they ran in circles. Enough said?

I quote Mom often when preaching at funerals, for she'd regularly tell me: "Don't you dare canonize me or say that you know I'm already in Heaven. Ask them to pray for my immortal soul"! A few weeks before her death during a visit, she suddenly asked: "What do you think God is like"?

While my mind raced between theological training and treasures of church teaching, and came up blank, she soon answered her question simply, and profoundly. "I think He's

GREAT"! That's Kass Quinlivan. And those of us who knew and loved her think that her God would say the same thing about her.

There's a Home, a place of perfect peace
...Home Sweet Home !

Chapter Twenty

A TRIPLE-LIFE STORY

One of the first thoughts that came to me in the moments after my mother died was that she had suffered three miscarriages after my brother Pat was born and before my sister Sue. We believe in our faith that from the moment of conception, human life begins and a soul exists, even when a tiniest child is created by God in the womb. In those days, the late 1950's, technology had not advanced to the point where it was easy to determine the gender of an embryonic life, so I'm pretty sure my parents didn't even know whether these three were boys or girls.

Eventually, a new medication was developed to help a woman carry her children to term, and the Lord blessed my parents with five more. Mom said that from her childhood she often said that she thought six would be a good number of children. When she married Dad, she was 30 years old and he 33. At that time, most of their siblings and peers had already married and were raising families. Mom and Dad taught us that you're better off waiting for the right person to marry; actually, it was always described as the one God had chosen for you. Mom had several offers to marry, but she waited for the right one and was always glad she did!

My three siblings who predeceased us were not discussed often, but from time to time we were reminded that my parents really had nine Quinlivan children. As a child, although mathematics was more a scourge rather than a gift. The thought of three more kids to share in chores and turns washing dishes seemed a real loss. Later in life, it dawned on me in a more mature way that my parents had lived with that loss in a faith-filled way. People can get so caught up in the broken hearts of loss that they might miss their own life's potential for joy. It's a kind of a cave that we have to work our way out of although it's tempting to remain and sometimes we might even think that we "forget" the lost ones. But they're not lost to God; they're safe.

When I was at St. Gregory the Great in Williamsville, we had a lovely young secretary in the Religious Education office who had one child, a boy about four years old. At one point, we rejoiced with her in the news that she and her husband were expecting again. They dearly longed to add to their family and, like many couples, didn't want too many years between their children. This time, God was apparently helping them quickly catch up on His command to "be fruitful and multiply" for they had conceived triplets! In a large parish, it's quite common to see young couples over the years going through the stages of family growth. As a celibate priest, the joy of new life and the privilege of baptizing the newest members of the parish family is a particular joy.

In March of that year, the parish was holding a St. Patrick's Day party. Of course, they didn't have to twist my arm to attend. As I may have mentioned, Msgr. Rupert Wright, our pastor used to kid me that my clothing consisted of two colors…clergy black and every shade of green. 'Twas true…and still is.

Toward the end of the St. Paddy's Day celebration, a call came on the parish's emergency pager. I ran out into the hall to check the message, and found that it was Heather from

Religious Ed. She had gone into labor prematurely and was at Sisters of Charity Hospital. The triplets were coming early— very early. And the doctors were trying to stop the labor, for at this number of weeks' gestation, these three precious babies would not be expected to survive. Heather asked me pointedly to come to the hospital and baptize them immediately after birth, and I raced to the car and headed to the maternity ward, praying all the way.

When I arrived, her parents and her in-laws were in the waiting room and hallways outside of the delivery room. Her husband, Chuck, was with her. My instruction was to be ready to be called in after the birth of each child. We didn't know if they would survive the birthing process, and all scientific methods could not assist them in breathing, for their little lungs were not yet developed enough to supply them with necessary oxygen.

My stomach churned with nervous anxiety. Not only did my heart break for this family, but my mind raced. What the heck do you say to people in this harrowing predicament?? All I could think of was the number of un-born children whose lives were terminated by legalized abortion. At the very same number of weeks since conception, they could legally be destroyed. And here we were, praying and hoping for a few moments of life as the process of labor was apparently not reversible at this point.

When the first child was born, I went in, took a little water, blessed it and baptized the baby. Then, it was back to the hallway to wait with the rest of the family. Within about 20 minutes, the other two were born and baptized. Then, the family invited me back into the room with them. Part of me was most terrified that I would be emotionally overwhelmed and useless in their presence, but as we went in, a beautiful aura of grace filled the room. The babies were still breathing, and nurses ever-so-gently kept listening to the tiny hearts with stethoscopes.

While three very tiny, approximately one-pound babies were being held and caressed, Heather introduced them: Lauren, Anthony and Joseph Frisicaro. What my fears had anticipated completely vanished in a room full of love and awe for how precious and fragile these too-small to thrive children were. Yes, the beauty and wonder of God's design, the fingers, tiny faces, ears and other features were intact, like ourselves at that stage in development, so many years ago.

The next memory will be with me all my life. Heather turned to me and asked "Would you like to hold her"? My heart stopped for a moment, as what struck me as the most generous offer of sharing I had ever known. This mother who knew that her baby would only live an hour or less was willing to share a precious moment with me. I couldn't say no, and took the baby in my hands. For only about thirty seconds, I admired and loved this little girl. Soon, I knew that I had been blessed, but that the parents and godparents really should be experiencing this.

In a little while, the nurses with stethoscopes confirmed that the life expectancy was accurate. As I recall, just under an hour since their birth, and in the exact order of birth, the three babies' hearts had stopped. We stayed a while, prayed a while, and eventually I decided that the family needed some private time. We briefly discussed a funeral Mass, and I left for the night.

The following day, I went to a Perpetual Eucharistic Adoration Chapel at St. Catherine of Siena church in West Seneca on my day off, to pray about how to approach preaching at such an unusual funeral. After some time in silence, immersed in the real presence of Christ, I felt free to weep a while with a mix of sorrow for lost life and immense, overwhelming gratitude to have witnessed such an amazing thing.

Soon, my tears were replaced by peace, and I began to ask the Lord how to express this whole range of feelings, and faith-inspired need to minister to the family and parish, and find the grace to do it effectively. What soon came to me was a simple matrix of unborn life, newborn life, sacramental life and eternal life. I had come so close to that process and been an instrument of what faith asks in Baptism, that a person be immersed in Christ who died and rose to eternal life. In this case, it was all encapsulated in just an hour or so.

Lyrics for a song started to flow, and after I wrote it down, I went into the sanctuary of the church where an electric keyboard stood waiting for me. I had my micro-cassette recorder in my backpack with my prayer books, and set it on the piano as I played until a melody was born. When the song was in its basic form of "finished," I went home to bed.

This is the lyric, recorded on a CD during my time with St. Lukes' Voices of Mercy.

LIFE TO LIFE

Born from Life into life
Precious, tiny babies
Born one Winter night
You came too soon to fight
Gifts received, and taken
Heaven's only light.

By storms of grief we're tossed
For all that we have lost
But we walk by faith in the author of life
And pray for healing.
We may not understand,
But we held you in our hands
An hour of holy hello, and swift good-bye.

Baptized into life,
By Father, Son and Spirit
Delivered from a world in strife
Bathed in the water of life
Fragile human pilgrims,
Grace multiplied by three,
Kissed into eternity.
So wrap us, O Lord in hope
Through this chapter of our story,
Our souls united, we long for the day
When you reveal your Glory.

Born again to full life
Silently escorted
on Angel of Mercy wings
To the Kingdom where Christ
Promised each a welcome
Before Our Father's face
Everlasting peaceful embrace,
Life to Life to Life by God's grace
Life to Life to Life…by God's grace…

Chapter Twenty-One

PUTTING FLESH ON THE FUNNY BONE?

Those of us who have the gene (or disorder?) that naturally drives us to tickle the funny bone can easily be labeled as attention-seekers, desperately insecure and needing affirmation. Yeah? So…tell me something I don't know about myself! Humorists are also called by God to give this human experience some light and silly moments, when we all know that taking life too seriously can be fatal and a sense of humor can be life-saving.

Sometimes, growing up in a household of wise-cracking people, I forget that there are those in the world who cannot appreciate attempts at humor. They might turn to you with disgust chiseled into their faces and say "What are you, a *comedian*"?? As if being a comedian isn't a noble profession. Historically, court jesters were vital to keeping the king from chopping off people's heads. They acted like God doesn't have a sense of humor—perish the thought!!

My friends have come to expect a certain style of commentary on something as simple as going out to lunch. The waiter or waitress says "Our special tonight is smothered chicken…" and I can't help but respond: "Ugh! Don't **tell** me how you killed it---just call it chicken. All I can picture is somebody holding a pillow over the little beak…it seems so cruel… I can see now how people become vegetarians. But then, we do peel, chop up, and boil the vegetables, and that *hardly* seems polite"! Then there are riffs on other dishes:

> Battered Fish: "Poor things need a **support group**, not **tartar sauce**"!
> Pulled Pork: " What? You think they're going to walk *willingly* into the slaughterhouse"?

Or my theory that all waiters and waitresses are all from the same family: "My name is Lucy Ifyuneedanything." "Amazing," I say, "last week our waiter was George Ifyuneedanything, on Sunday, it was "Latasha Ifyuneedanything. Such a perfect, descriptive last name…they are true servants, that Ifyuneedanything family"!

My alternative response is more sarcastic: "Your name is Suzie if we need anything. What is your name if we **don't** need anything"? I pass when the entrée includes artichokes. My Irish superstition kicks in. Why even attempt to eat something with "choke" in the title? It's a set-up. Paging Dr. Heimlich…

Jesus does have a sense of humor. I'm reminded of it every day. And because He is rich in mercy and forgiveness, I prefer to believe that He thinks I'm hilarious. And I, Him! Do you really think that He could call together disciples who were fishermen, former prostitutes, and tax collectors and not keep them amused somehow as they walked from town to town? Wouldn't it make sense that while He was revealing the glory of the Kingdom and the love of the Heavenly Father, that He often smiled and laughed at how ridiculous our ways of thinking and acting can be?

I always say that while He taught His friends humility, He was acutely aware that humor and humility come from the same linguistic root. My sense as I journey with the Lord is that the most important thing that He can teach me is to laugh at myself. Especially when I get down on myself and want to beat myself up for being weak, having faults, and being prone to sin. Christ never hates a sinner, but he preaches that we should hate sin so as to avoid it with all our strength. Then, His amazing grace and our will begin working together in new directions.

Many, many times, Jesus taught that we should not judge. One particular day, He used a device in every humorist's tool belt: exaggeration. "Remove the beam in your own eye before you point out the splinter in your brother's". When I first discovered that this had to be a teaching moment in laughing at yourself, I asked my friend Debbie Keenan to make me a plank. I had recently been asked to give a talk on God's sense of humor, and Debbie is a very gifted, creative visual artist. She made me a small, lightweight plank that I could hide behind my back as I read that Gospel passage to begin the talk.

I then instructed the audience to close their eyes and try to imagine their own spiritual eye-planks or splinters. While their eyes were close, I carefully attached the six-inch "beam" to my glasses, then announced: "Okay, open your eyes"! and slowly turn sideways for maximum effect. ("Beam me eye, Scotty!?)" It's helpful to picture Jesus preaching on those hills and mountainsides using big, bold gestures like a stage actor playing to the last row. And, there were no sound systems, of course. In my mind, in between the awe-inspiring and profoundly moving words of the Word made flesh, his words could also make a point and get a smile or laugh with holy tongue in cheek, or a wink to those attuned to his humor.

We must be careful not to sanitize and solemnize the wit that accompanies Christ's wisdom. When He speaks the woes to the Pharisees, He adds a great kind of slapstick image: "You strain out the gnat and swallow a camel"! Jesus probably loves camels, for they brought the Magi to His nativity and His Gospel brings these most unusual-looking beasts to our attention. Try picturing one working on trying to get through the eye of a needle without smiling. (Okay, scripture scholars say that there was actually a space between two hills called "the needle's eye pass" where camels could hardly get through. So this is actually a pun; what some call the lowest form of humor. Punning is an affliction of personality that I suffer from... or rather, thoroughly enjoy despite the fact that others claim to suffer from my puns. So—now I can defend myself that Jesus did it...so it's actually Christian tradition!)

Have you ever stopped to ponder that St. Peter was really in his impetuosity a bit of a pratfall artist? Here's this apostle in the boat when Jesus comes up, walking on water, inviting him to join in the promenade. The one Christ nicknamed the "rock" soon begins to sink like a stone, and Peter panics. So, let me get this straight: Jesus chose a fisherman who can't swim to lead the Church. This scenario just reminds me a bit too much of the Island of Misfit Toys in *Rudolph, the Red-Nose Reindeer.* And the b-b-b-b-boat that can't stay a-f-f-f-f-float, or the bird that can't fly. "I swim"! he announces, diving into a bowl of water. (Side note: ever notice the tragic ending of that animated classic? When Santa's elves are giving each toy an umbrella and dropping them from the sleigh, an ignorant elf holds back on an umbrella for the bird who can't fly. He went down....in history. Or rather, *he* went down and *was* history....)

Researching the topic of God's sense of humor, I found several books that gave me much material for the talk on Holy Humor. One author wrote of an early tradition in Christian history which joyously celebrated a special day of laughter and merriment on Easter Monday. Because God literally gets the last laugh on sin and death through the Resurrection (and He will, ultimately, when Christ returns), believers would hire clowns and employ humor and play, to bring some healthy, holy levity to Easter's exaltation. How I wish we could revive that tradition! Jesus says we should approach the Father like children, and kids need the element of play to spark imagination, problem-solving enjoying the gift of giggles.

A quote attributed to St. Teresa of Avila quickly became one of my favorites: "From somber, serious, and sullen saints…save us, O Lord"! My Amen couldn't be louder. And my desire to integrate some laughter into every day couldn't be a more seriously sacred calling, even when the joke falls flat and the intended audience remains stone-faced and dreadfully un-moved. Laughter has been called "temporary anesthesia of the heart". Isn't it true that you cannot enjoy a good laugh with someone and still consider him/her an enemy??

The late Cardinal Seunens once said that we are called God's chosen people, but often we act more like His *frozen* people. Have you ever noticed how far back or far away some church-goers sit from others? Where did Jesus say "Where two or more are *scattered* in my name, I am in the midst of them"? You know how you can identify the Catholics at a backyard picnic? They put their lawn chairs in your neighbor's yard. When the preacher asks a question such as "Why is Sunday a day of rest"? and a small child answers "Because so many people fall asleep in church", we have some work to do!

Admittedly, the celebrational style of me and my priest brothers might contribute to this. At one time in my home parish, we had a priest who prided himself on having the fastest celebrations. Before DVD players had fast forward, we had this priest who could finish a Sunday liturgy in 24 minutes. One could get the sense at the end of the prayers that he read with great speed that a response more fitting than "Amen" would be "SOLD-- to the little lady with the green rosary"! Going once, going twice, going overboard?? My brother Joe and I were altar boys at one of his Masses, and when we processed into the sacristy after Mass this priest actually said "Ah---twenty six minutes. It's communion that takes all the time"!

Lectors can bring an important lay ministry into the mix by proclaiming the readings. But they can also bring distraction through mispronouncing words. The reading was from the Book of Sirach, not Xerox. There were caravans of camels, not carmels. And the most-repeated and universal flub "the Lord sent Moses a pillar of fire and burning brazier". It's pronounced *bray*-zur otherwise it sounds like Moses inspired the Women's Liberation movement of the 1960's and 70's. The new translation says fire pot...that's easier for readers to say without confusion.

At Christmas, those proclaiming the Gospel have to be sure to pause at the commas, because the literalists in the congregation hear "The shepherds went to Bethlehem and found Mary and Joseph and the infant lying in the manger". Wow---close family. I try to pause longer: "Mary and Joseph.... (one-two-three-four) **and** the baby lying in the manger".

I read somewhere that Abraham and Sarah's late-in-life son Isaac means **God's laugh**. Genesis 21:6 has Sarah speaking these important words of inspiration: "God has given me cause to laugh....all who hear of it will laugh with me". Long before television producers realized that we could enjoy the funniest home movies, God undoubtedly started collecting them. I can't wait to get to that screening room, and I'm quite sure that some of my most embarrassing moments might make the program!

Popes can be funny, too. In the process of approving blueprints for a new building on the grounds of the Vatican, Pope John XXIII smiled and handed the plans back to the architect with the words 'Non sumus angeli' (We're not angels). The planning team held an emergency meeting to figure out what these profound spiritual words might mean. Did he want more angel wings in the design? Should they have included a confessional? No---another set of eyes looked at the drawings and realized that there were no restrooms in the place.

The most serious moments can bring about our greatest challenges to unintentional humor. When my friend Mike Carabelli's mother died, there was a song that Bette Midler had recorded called *"My Mother's Eyes."* The elderly pastor agreed to let them play it as a meditation song after communion. But the young altar servers were not familiar with the album's order of songs. After a moment of great and prayerful silence, he dropped the needle on the wrong song: Midler's lively cover version of the Andrews Sisters' classic *Boogie Woogie Bugle Boy*! I found the irony irresistible, and couldn't help but picture his mother, Eleanor, preferring to do a jitterbug in paradise than listen to a sentimental ballad!

Young children have a penchant for speaking what they think, until we teach them to edit their thoughts. A few years ago, after a Sunday Mass I was in the sacristy changing from a simple white vestment to a white stole for a scheduled Baptism. Just outside the sacristy door, two small girls about the age of four or five were watching me. I did not recognize them, so I figured that they had come in with visitors and family for the Baptism. As I pulled off my outer vestment, one of them spoke up; "That's a pretty *princess dress* you're wearing!" I briefly took offense, rolling my eyes as I turned to the vestment case to find the stole. Then I politely turned to the kids, smiling through gritted teeth: "You can go sit with your families now"! In pastoral counseling, they call a too-serious and non-responsive facial expression a "flat affect," which is often a sign of depression. Depression is no laughing matter, but healing and recovery are often signified in the breaking of a smile and or chuckle. I pray that you and I might never lose our ability and need to play.

Come join the Prodigal Parade, cast impropriety to the past
New shoes on your feet, Dad has killed the fattened calf
It's a joyful jig we're dancing when we've come to our senses at last!

For some reason, when leading Penance Services, prayer gatherings to prepare people for confession, I often infuse some humor. When I was writing songs for my CD collection with the theme of Divine Mercy, I came up with the idea for *Prodigal Parade*. Perhaps I had seen too many re-runs of Hollywood musical production numbers filmed on back-lots with throngs of people joining and swelling the crowd. But the idea of every forgiven sinner being part of that kind of group activity made sense.

To some, looking for a serene and meditative musical prayer to touch their soul like a feather from an angel's wing…it has to be jarring. The song starts with a drum track like a marching band, the kind that help bring a rah-rah feel to football games. As a pastor, I sometimes think that the "coach" of the souls entrusted to me has to reach for fresh approaches to get people's attention and then turn it to the One who offers them saving grace. Admittedly, the ambitious linebacker in me sometimes crosses a line or two, and the whistle blows: offsides! So then, I simply need to ask forgiveness…and I find out whether or not it's been learned by the ones who hear the words of Jesus and follow him.

A few years ago, we held an Easter season dance at the Blessed Sacrament parish center and called it the "Prodigal Prom." The concept was like the day of laughter of old, something akin to what Polish Americans (at least in Buffalo) call Dyngus Day; festive music, food, and games on the day after Easter, to extend the celebration. The "prom" idea may have brought back too many memories of polyester tuxedos or the heart-break of not being invited by the one who you were convinced was your soul-mate. But those of us who showed up had great fun. We projected the image of Divine

Mercy on the wall, with red and white balloons under the rays of the same colors emanating from Jesus's pierced heart. All during Lent, we passed out "tickets" to every person who went to Confession and invited them to celebrate being forgiven with joyful dance. It was worth a try. And nobody had to rent a tuxedo, rent a limo, or worry if they didn't have a date.... Like David, we danced before God. Admittedly, to different music and thankfully, with much more clothing than he.

Chapter Twenty-Two

GOIN' OUT

Everybody has some kind of calling from God, but being called and gifted is just the beginning. One of my favorite sayings is that the Lord doesn't call the equipped, He equips the called. But logically the next step after being called is being sent. The cliché when award nominations are announced says "It's an honor just to be nominated!" But they never ask the winners if they accept the responsibility that comes with being chosen and singled out. Seems to be that there are so many awards shows and super games in sports that the average person only recalls the names of the winner for a few days anyway. The fifteen minutes of fame that Andy Warhol spoke of (in *his* fifteen minutes...) seems to be true.

Of course, in the life of faith this analogy only goes so far. The called, the chosen, those who profess and believe, who make commitments, also agree to go where we're sent. Priests and sisters get used to moving every several years, and while that might tempt some not to emotionally invest in the community and its members while anticipating an eventual transfer, seems to be too safe an option!

Goin' Out

҂ᷧ҂ᷧ҂ᷧ҂ᷧ҂ᷧ҂ᷧ

We're **Goin' Out**, with Jesus in the lead…
We'll never doubt, never doubt, never doubt…
'Cuz He knows our every need
We're gonna never think of leavin'
We're gonna run this race believin'
'Cuz there's so much more life to live
As His river of grace is poured
And we're called to go and give…
We're **Goin' Out** to serve our Lord!!

Mama, don't you worry, 'bout my wand'ring in the night
my Heavenly Father sent the angels
to guide my path, to keep it right.
Daddy don't be frettin'…I promise not to waste my time
with the Lord there's no forgettin'…
there's Holy Mountains left to climb!

Because the vowed and promised celibates and virgins have promised obedience to the ones who help discern *where* we're called next, after they affirm *that* we're called to that particular vocation, and we need to trust that process. It's an honor to be nominated but sometimes it's a cross to be transferred!

In my mind, I keep going back to the fact that our sacramental rituals each end with a sending forth, a dismissal. "Go in peace, the Mass is ended", or "Go and sin no more"! Being sent out, going out, as my lyric proclaims, has to become second nature for Christians. Missionaries are sent with blessings to faraway lands, Jesus gave specific orders to his Apostles (the very name means *sent*) of what to bring and what not to bring. Simple instructions actually, were the first sendings, and Christ was quite clear in not being over-burdened with material things. (My Irish guilt immediately reminds me of the boxes of things that move with me from parish to parish and remain un-touched. My seminary class notes are still with me, though the light of day has not found them in about twenty years! With all due respect to my professors who are still living and by strange coincidence might actually read this book, I haven't saved the notes for high, scholastic purposes. I just can't part with the comments and cartoons in the side columns of the oh-so-serious theological notes…you know…in case I ever write a book…)

On a few occasions, such as the installation of a new diocesan bishop or papal election, I have been called upon to do what they call "color commentary" on the local television stations. Never do I miss the irony that thirty years ago, upon graduation from college with my Bachelor of Arts degree in Journalism, Broadcasting and Speech, my resume was sent to each of these places many times. I would apply for every job opening advertised in the Want Ads at TV stations. Now suddenly I'm remembering things more clearly. Let me clarify that. I applied for **both** of the positions I saw advertised in the five long years of hoping for a career in television! There were so few. And much of hiring was by word of mouth, and the mouths I knew *never* spoke the words: "Welcome to the station! Here's your desk"! (I did, however, achieve part-time news writer status for that one year. Not exactly the stuff the Buffalo Broadcasting Hall of Fame looks for, but it would certainly be a *miracle* to be nominated for a part-time position thirty years ago!)

As a priest, on camera, it's important to keep in mind the dignity of the ordained state. But as a comedy writer and smart-aleck Irishman, I also remember my theories of Jesus' sense of humor. Many actors say that their best performances end up on the cutting room floor victims of film editors' whims. One memory I have of being taped for a local news show was March 13, 2013, the day Pope Francis was elected. They sat me in front of a large flat-screen TV with a live feed from Vatican City, St. Peter's Basilica. Then they shot me watching the television as we awaited the newly-announced Holy Father to make his first appearance. One of my unspoken thoughts (despite popular opinion, there are a few...) was that my mother was wrong. She always told us we'd never get anywhere in life if we sat in front of the TV all day. Well, all those years of practice came in handy that day, and I was obviously a skilled viewer, for they were videotaping me watching TV. Great gig if you can get it!!

While we waited for the curtains to part, it struck me that our first South American Pope might have a sense of humor like mine. If he were a fan of Andrew Lloyd Webber and Tim Rice, I suggested that he might walk through the curtain and sing "Don't cry for me, Catholic people"! I didn't even get a chance to share the line my sister Mary came up with when a seagull perched itself on the chimney of the Sistine chapel as the world's visual media zoomed in, awaiting white smoke. She quipped "He can wait all day, but he can't get into the conclave, he's *not a cardinal*"!

Chapter Twenty-Three

ORDINATION DAY

The sun rose at its scheduled hour on April 29, 1995. South Buffalo was arrayed in Easter joy, and St. Teresa's was prepared for a celebration that had not taken place in its sacred space in it's almost one hundred years---the ordination of a priest. The Sacrament of Holy Orders was scheduled for me through the office of our then-bishop, Most Rev. Edward D. Head, D.D. From my earliest recollections of a sense of being called to this appointed, anointed day, it was approximately thirty years. I recently discovered that my home parish was consecrated on April 29, 1900, ninety-five years earlier to the day. The parish opened in 1897, but the tradition of consecrating it is tied to the building costs being paid in full.

One year earlier, when my classmates and I graduated from Christ the King Seminary and were presented with our Masters of Divinity degrees, we were soon to be ordained as Transitional Deacons. It's the last step toward priesthood, and for one year we would then be living in a parish full-time and preparing for the transition into ministry as priests of Jesus Christ.

Ordination Day

❦❦❦❦❦

When you called my name,
something deep inside me
Trembled as I recognized Truth
Would I take the chance,
could I have this dance
Heard within my soul,
from my youth

Here I am, you called me.
Help my heart to trust in your voice
Here we go, take me, Jesus
Amen, let it be, is my choice

As I now respond to the mystery
Daily persevere, die and rise
Prostrate on the ground,
as your grace abounds
Come, O Spirit, make me wise

Here I am, you called me….

Jesus, you ordain, share your ministry
With a man who doesn't deserve
(but) in my yes, they might see
Holy mystery
That for your greater glory I serve.

Here I am, you called me…

Graduation day, for all the years of study and spiritual formation, writing papers and working at "field assignments" for practicum purposes, was greatly anticipated. But, to be honest, I never felt called by God to receive a Master's Degree in Divinity. It was required for candidates seeking ordination, and I participated in it to the best of my abilities. While another diploma was nice, the experiences my soul longed to enter would begin ordination day, and beyond.

As I've said earlier in this book, being from a large family, one sometimes has a penchant to stand out, to be a bit different, to be known for yourself and not just blend into the crowd. Seminaries in my part of the world are rarely so crowded that one has to make much effort to be an individual. When I began my studies at Christ the King, the student body of men preparing for priestly ministry numbered approximately forty. Many other lay students were seeking degrees for pastoral ministry as well, and they added diverse perspectives for us, much of the time keeping us from feeling like a few guys in a fishbowl.

There was one special surprise on graduation day, when the mail arrived and I received a congratulatory telegram from Joan Rivers! While it had been years since my last submission of one-liners, she had insisted when we met two years earlier backstage at Shea's Buffalo Theater that I let her know when I was graduating. So in March or April, I sent off a letter to notify her, and pretty much thank her for keeping me encouraged to seek my life's purpose by purchasing jokes from an unknown kid from South Buffalo. With my letter, I felt like I was acknowledging an era in my life where humor helped save my sanity. There was a sense of closure, and I was delighted to move on.

When the mail came, I was as tickled as I was the day the first check for $20 arrived when Joan bought two jokes. It was like an old friend waving as you drive away on moving day. Or, as Bob Hope used to say "Thanks for the memories!" My humor came in handy during seminary days. For special occasions, when there was a need for an entertainment committee, I always signed up. I wrote what I thought were some pretty clever song parodies and pulled together a group of singing seminarians to go for a laugh or three. The subject matter was strictly inside humor, and one-time yucks. My favorite was a ten-minute skit for the orientation weekend when we welcomed new seminarians each year. It was called "No Cassock Park," a take-off on a box office bonanza that summer about Dinah Shore...on no, now I remember---dinosaurs!

There was a wonderful nun who worked in the Library, Sr. Mary Tiburtia Gorecki. She had a great sense of humor, and agreed to play herself as a guardian angel. Every time she made her entrance from the side of the stage, one of the seminarians would throw a handful of glitter to announce her arrival. She played every line like Lucille Ball in her prime, and the audience loved it. A guardian angel was the perfect role for Sr. Tibertia. She not only offered motherly advice to seminarians overwhelmed with academic stress, she also forgave more overdue library book fees than she ever collected. Hopefully, every seminarian who ever became a pastor at a church with a school will remember *that* when parents were late with tuition payments.

When the years of theological studies seemed to make one's ordination day seem light-years away, Sr. T. would talk turkey. "Hey," she'd say with a twinkle in her eye "God wants you to be a priest and you're gonna be great, and I'm gonna pray that you pass all those tests. You will. You'll see"! That kind of sweet wisdom was a balm to eyestrain from hundreds of pages of reading assignments. It was like the voice of God Himself reminding you whose idea this whole priesthood idea was in the first place.

Ordination day was like a spiritual episode of the classic TV program *This is Your Life*. In bygone years, many young men entered seminary directly from high school, or right from 8th Grade into what they called "minor seminary." My generation came to the formation process with a list of former employers, addresses, and a few, with former fiancées. We were given a choice by the Diocese whether to be ordained at our beautiful cathedral of St. Joseph in downtown Buffalo or at our own parish church. For me, there was no other option than St. Teresa's. I had literally grown up in the parish church, school, and parish center. My fingerprints were all over the place, but, more importantly, God's fingerprints were, too. I figured that I would have the rest of my life to celebrate special events at the cathedral, and subsequently I have. But the home parish was the obvious choice, and a great place to begin my new life.

My parents were married there in 1953, and five of their six children were Baptized there (my Canadian birthplace made me the only non-St. Teresa Baptism) Countless thousands of memories and experiences of the Lord's grace happened for me in St. Teresa's. That day in April, 1995, the bishop would silently lay his hands on my head and invoke the Holy Spirit, and I would become part of a tradition of ordained ministry in the Catholic faith. Before the laying of hands, however, the candidate for ordination lies prostrate on the floor before the altar while the congregation invoked the Saints of heaven in a Litany of Saints. What moved me especially is that the place on the carpet where I would lie in prayer and prostration happened to be the spot where my father's casket had been at his funeral; only a few feet from the altar rail where I made my First Eucharist in 1968. And several yards from the baptismal font where I first stood as godfather for my nephew, Kevin in 1984.

My memories of ordination day can be compared to spiritual surfing. The expectation, joy, and a mix and myriad of emotions were the wave, and I was Moon-Doggie of the old Frankie and Annette movies, riding the wave every surfer dreams about all his life. I was aware, from my pre-ordination years, that I would enter the church that day and an hour and a half later, leave with orders to serve. Holy Orders is what we call the sacrament. While the surfing analogy works to a point (although I must admit I have never set foot on a surfboard...) deep-sea diving also works. In your spirit, you are plunged into a depth of God's grace and made aware at the core of your being that you'll need a life-line to go deeper and do what your Creator has planned.

The mind gets a panoramic view of your life on a day like ordination day. Looking around the church, the mix of family and friends was so uplifting and affirming. People from the various parishes where I lived and worked as a seminarian were there, with the faithful St. Teresa's ladies and gents from daily Mass. My friends from choir, the people with whom I worked Bingo, co-workers from Mercy Hospital and various other jobs that I had held on the way to this day. The revolving door of vocational confusion that perplexed me in my twenties had finally ceased. The "Poor Bill" label would disappear as my calling came to the moment of transition through sacramental grace and commitment. And on this day, I could look around and be more grateful than I can probably ever explain.

Every April 29th since, I have made an effort to stop back to St. Teresa's and pray a while. In some ways, as I'm sure married people would agree, it doesn't feel like as many years as the calendar tells me. I can still picture my god-parents/cousins Aileen and Jim carrying the gifts of bread and wine in the procession. The choir, made up of a vast mix of musicians that I'd played and sung with over the years, was off to the left. My mother, sisters, and brothers were on the left, in the front.

At an ordination, the candidate first takes his place in the front pew with his family. At a certain moment early in the ceremony, there is a calling forth, and you stand, proclaiming

"Present!" when called, and step forward before the Lord, the Bishop, and the Church to make sacred promises.

In the Roman Catholic Church, a priest's hands are anointed with Sacred Chrism, one of the holy oils used for Sacraments. Bishop Head was a very tall man, and his hands were gigantic by most standards. So when he laid his hands on any head, even with an extra-large head like mine, you were covered. When he anointed my hands, he spread the oil generously in a full sacramental sign! There's a old tradition where the candidate's hands used to be wrapped after anointing with a white cloth called in Latin a *maniturgium* (which literally means, hand towel). After the anointing, the newly-ordained priest would process solemnly into the sacristy and work the oil into his hands, then dry them with the cloth. The pious tradition then had the family keep the cloth for the mother of the newly ordained's burial, and her hands would be wrapped with it as the mother of a priest. And there's a sweet devotional belief that the Virgin Mary, Mother of Christ the High Priest, would un-wrap it for her as she entered Heaven.

At the time of my class being ordained, this tradition had fallen out of practice. In later years, the practice has occasionally been revived. That's okay, though. When my mother died, she wouldn't have needed to tell one more living person that her son was a priest. She took the opportunity to tell anyone who would listen, whenever opportunity knocked. And if it didn't, *she* knocked and told them anyway. Mom told me later that my ordination day was one of the most beautiful in her life as I'm sure the parents of priests often say. When you consider the period of "engagement" from application to ordination, in my case about six years, it's a long wait. And when you wander and wonder as many years as I did before calling for a first vocation interview that adds years to the waiting.

But the wait ended on a gorgeous Saturday morning in 1995. And the journey has continued, adding stories and adventures in ministry ever since. This book has been my chance to share some of those experiences, which helped me truly find my song. My hope is that those who have yet to discover their vocation will keep searching until they find exactly how they've been *Made to Praise Him*. And our mighty God's ears delight to receive the melody of His love singing through us all—throughout the world and into the Kingdom!

Photo Album

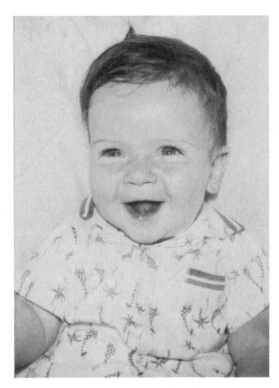

Toothless me at about six months, 1960.
Happy and oblivious to the cowlick in my
hair. It remains to this day!

So serious as I become a US citizen at age 3

Siblings in pre-Brady bunch era. (L to R: Back row; Sue, Eileen, Pat. Front; Joe, Mary, Bill)

The posing stairway at our homestead, 205 Stevenson St., S. Buffalo

Fr. John Kilian and his altar boy after my First Mass

Senior portrait, Bishop
Timon High School, 1978.

Stalked the tour bus, got my photo with
Marie Osmond, 1984

Collecting paychecks and paper cuts as a Medical
Record Filer

On the set of "The Natural," Robert Redford
movie shot in Buffalo, 1983. Waiting for my
close-up. Officially costumed in a zoot suit

Can we talk? Met Joan Rivers backstage at Shea's
Buffalo Theater, 1992. Three times she said "Let
me know when you graduate (seminary)!"

Lying prostrate in prayer on Ordination Day, at St. Teresa's, my spiritual home for most of my life!

Bishop Edward D. Head invokes the Holy Spirit to ordain me a priest of Jesus Christ

The first day Mom can say to everyone she meets, "Did I tell you my son's a priest?"

First blessing for the lady who gave me birth and so much more. Dad watched from the Kingdom!
(April 29, 1995)

The late, great Fr. Merrick J. Bednar, at my ordination reception

First encounter with Sr. Briege McKenna, OSC at priest conference, Franciscan University at Steubenville, 1997

Haven't met Julie Andrews yet, but pretended to during Salzburg, Austria "Sound of Music Bus Tour"

A jump for joy, on the very road where Maria sings "I Have Confidence." Julie Andrews did it with a guitar case and carpet bag

Priest brothers/friends (L to R: Fr. Peter Karalus, the author, Fr. Dan Young, Fr. Leon Biernat, Fr. Joseph Bertha)

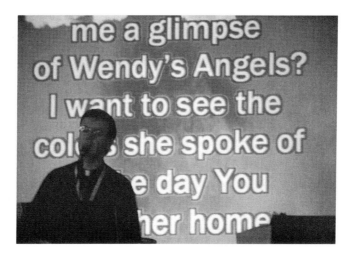

Singing at the Kingdom Bound Christian Music Festival

With my holy
friend Wendy Rose
Marks, Pentecost
1999

On outdoor stage at World Youth Day, Toronto,
2002 with Ireland's musical royalty, DANA

The "Buffalo Boys" and the "Twins." Fr. Joseph Bertha and I with Dublin's Triona (right) and Gemma (left) King

Singing with DANA (right) and Heather Boctor Schieder, pro-life song "This Is My Body." An almost out-of-body spiritual experience!

Honored to share "Priest of Mine" at International Priest retreat in Ars, France. Photo copyright Dominique Lefevre, 2009

Video shoot for "Advent Wreath Carol," 2007.
Photo by Brandon Lata.

Me and Benny the Wonder Dog meet St. Nicholas
(Chris Kolb)

After outdoor procession with Blessed
Sacrament in Ars, walk-same path at St. John
Vianney. With Cathi Brenti (Center, Beatitudes
Community, retreat coordinator), Fr. Bertha.

MercySongs/MercyPrayers photo shoot, 2011. Photo by Brandon Lata

About the Author

Fr. Bill Quinlivan has recorded seven CDs of original songs, and this volume includes the back-stories of many of his compositions. Before becoming a priest, he was a comedy writer, aspiring screenwriter, and worked in radio. For a time he served as a portrait photographer as well as a stint as a government employee at the IRS. He now works for the "perfect boss." The BIG boss!! Fr. Bill is the fourth-born Quinlivan, raised in predominately Irish Catholic South Buffalo. But his first fifty years have taken him to other corners of the world. He is currently pastor of Blessed Sacrament Parish in the Town of Tonawanda, New York, in the Diocese of Buffalo. He was ordained in 1995, and in addition to his diocesan assignments is involved at St. Luke's Mission of Mercy on Buffalo's East Side, a ministry to the homeless and addicted. He still finds songs coming from his heart when he prays, and is delighted to encourage others to "find their song" in God's plan. A lot of faith and a sense of humor always help!